L. Gautier, Digby S. Wrangham, de Saint-Victor Adam

The Liturgical Poetry of Adam of Saint Victor

Vol. 1

L. Gautier, Digby S. Wrangham, de Saint-Victor Adam

The Liturgical Poetry of Adam of Saint Victor
Vol. 1

ISBN/EAN: 9783337777692

Printed in Europe, USA, Canada, Australia, Japan

Cover: Foto ©Thomas Meinert / pixelio.de

More available books at **www.hansebooks.com**

THE LITURGICAL POETRY

OF

ADAM OF ST. VICTOR.

FROM THE TEXT OF GAUTIER.

WITH TRANSLATIONS INTO ENGLISH IN THE ORIGINAL METRES
AND SHORT EXPLANATORY NOTES BY

DIGBY S. WRANGHAM, M.A.,

ST. JOHN'S COLLEGE, OXFORD,

Vicar of Darrington, Yorkshire.

VOL. I.

LONDON:

KEGAN PAUL, TRENCH, & CO., 1, PATERNOSTER SQUARE.

MDCCCLXXXI.

TO

HIS ROYAL HIGHNESS

PRINCE LEOPOLD,

DUKE OF ALBANY, EARL OF CLARENCE,

BARON ARKLOW, K.G., K.T., G.C.M.G., G.C.S.I.,

&c. &c. &c.,

LIKE HIS ILLUSTRIOUS AND GIFTED FATHER,

A SCHOLAR AND PATRON OF LETTERS,

THIS ATTEMPT

TO

ILLUSTRATE AND INTERPRET

A GREAT MEDIÆVAL CLASSIC

IS

WITH HIS PERMISSION

DEDICATED

BY ONE WHO, UNLIKE HIS ROYAL HIGHNESS, CANNOT

HOPE TO ENHANCE,

BUT ONLY FEARS TO FORFEIT,

THE REPUTATION FOR GRACEFUL SCHOLARSHIP

THAT IN DAYS GONE BY

DISTINGUISHED THE NAME HE BEARS.

PREFACE.

IN offering this work to the public I am breaking what is practically new ground to the great majority of English readers. The circumstances, detailed in the Introduction to M. Gautier's Edition, under which the larger part of the poetry of Adam of St. Victor was entirely lost to the world for many years after the French Revolution, seem likely to give an interest and novelty to it in this country at this day, which that Edition, published in Paris in 1858-59, has only to a very limited degree forestalled. I feel therefore that, so far as the original text is concerned, I am doing good service to the lovers of Mediæval Hymnology, by rendering it more accessible to them in this, the first edition of it published in England.

As regards what forms the principal part of my work in these volumes, viz., the Translations, I feel, on the other hand, that much apology is due for the imperfections with which I know they abound, and I am anxious therefore to explain the principles which have guided me in my attempts—for they are no better than attempts—to render the original into our tongue.

I have looked at the duty of a translator as analogous to that of an engraver, and felt that, the poet being a "word-*painter*," the translator must be a "word-*engraver*"; in other words, that to be successful, he must reproduce faithfully, as a whole and in detail, what he sets himself to copy. A so-called translation, which is stripped at the taste of the translator not only of the *form* of the original, viz., its metre, but more or less also of the thoughts and expressions with which that form is clothed, appears to me to fail to be what it professes to be, just in proportion as these defects, if I may venture to call them so, appear in it. It may be a very beautiful piece of poetry in itself,—and it very often is so,—but a *translation*, *i.e.*, a *transferring* of a given original from one language into another it can scarcely be. If I were to take the picture of a beautiful boy with curling locks and "fair and of a ruddy countenance," and draw another, as fancy led me, of that same boy in later life, bronzed in the battle of life, of stalwart form and with flowing beard; though I might keep the shapely features of the original face before me constantly and reproduce their outline carefully, no one could say that I had made a *copy* of the picture I had seen. Those who saw the two portraits together might detect that the child was the father of the man, but that would be all. They would count the two as separate works of art, standing or falling by their own several faults or merits, and never dream that the second was intended to reproduce the first.

And what is true of the copyist would seem to be necessarily still truer of the engraver, who has not the help of colours to aid his efforts, as the former has, and is compelled therefore to follow most closely his original both in outline and detail, if he would have that original recognizable at all in the sombrer hues of his engraving.

In like manner the translator, so far from needing the originality with which some would have him endowed, must be content, I submit, like the engraver, to follow his original painfully, line after line, and not be satisfied with his work till he has succeeded in so reconstructing it, as to leave no doubt upon the mind of the reader of the two works as to their inter-identity. In a certain sense, no doubt, an engraver should be an artist, that is to say, he should have a good eye for *proportion*, and be well versed in the rules of drawing generally; and in the same sense a translator should be something of a poet, with a good ear for rhythm,—the *proportion* of poetry,—and not ignorant of the rules of poetical composition. But neither engraver nor translator needs to be original, to my mind; for, when his *originality* comes in at the window, his *original* goes out at the door. It is a singular fact, for I think it is a fact, that great poets have not been very successful translators, nor successful translators very great poets. Exceptions there may have been to this rule, but very rare ones. The only great poet who was—I can scarcely say a great—but a good translator, that I can call to mind, was Dryden, and his translations are of the freest; while the merits of Milton, Pope, Cowper, Shelley and Keble, *as translators*, pale before those of Gifford, Neale, Frere and Conington.

Should I seem to go too far were I to suggest that the object of a translator and that of a parodist should be much the same in kind, however different in effect? The difference between them appears to me to be simply this, viz., that, while both preserve the metre of their original, the translator changes its language, and preserves, as far as possible, its meaning, and the parodist changes its meaning, and, as far as possible, preserves its language.

If in these principles, which I cannot help thinking ought to govern translators, I am at all right,—however imperfect may be, and are, my own attempts to carry them out,—I need scarcely point out how absolutely essential it is to observe them in translating such an author as Adam of St. Victor, because it is *manner* and not *matter* that is his distinguishing characteristic. As Archdeacon Cheetham observes in a private letter to me, "though his variations on his theme are almost always sweet, Adam's range is not great;" and, therefore, if you take away his metres, which are ever-changing in the same Sequence even, and his peculiar mode of building them up, till he finishes with a rush of liquid rhyme, you utterly efface what is his distinguishing feature. No author probably is so difficult to translate—such at least was Dr. Neale's opinion, and he had had experience enough of the difficulty to make him a judge;—but, if translated at all, it can only be fairly done by adhering strictly to the lines upon which Adam himself builds his mellifluous superstructure. It is better, to my fancy, to present even the skeleton of him, as one may hope to succeed in doing, in a perfectly literal translation; than to give him to the world as a shapeless mummy, embalmed though it may be in the richest spices of original thought and feeling.

At the same time I would not be understood to maintain that no license at all is permitted to the translator;—my own versions of Adam of St. Victor would be more faulty, than I quite feel they are as it is, were that the case. I simply urge that the license must at any rate be limited, in the case of additions or omissions, to such as leave intact the sense of the original passages, and, in the case of metres, to, at most, the occasional varying the rhythm of some of them, leaving the number of syllables the same. Such a metre as the following, *e.g.*,—and there are some four or five of that character in Adam's collection of sequences, appears to me to be one, that it is almost impossible in our consonant-ridden language to reproduce faithfully and yet gracefully.

> Salve, dies dierum gloria,
> Dies felix, Christi victoria,
> Dies digna jugi lætitia.
> Dies prima!

I have ventured, therefore, to alter the emphasis, while keeping intact the length, of each line, thus:

> Hail, day, the glory of all days! to thee!
> Thrice happy day, Christ's day of victory!
> The first day, day most fit continually
> Our joy to show!

I have adopted the same course, and for the same reason, in the case of four other Sequences, viz.: "Gaude Sion, quæ diem recolis;" "Jerusalem et Sion filiæ;" "Aquas plenas amaritudine;" and "Gratiani grata solempnitas." A few lines, sprinkled about here and there in other Sequences, I have treated in the same way. With these exceptions, I have kept, I believe, rigidly to the exact metre of each original Sequence.

One great difficulty in carrying out the principle of literal translation in these volumes has been, not only the number, but the character also, of the rhymes so called for. English rhymes are naturally, and generally, *single* rhymes; Latin rhymes, on the other hand, are naturally, and generally, *double* rhymes. In Latin, again, the same terminations, if attached to words of different meanings, are held to rhyme; in English, however, this is not the case,—every word, in order to make a good rhyme, must in our language have a different termination, ultimate or penultimate,—according as the rhyme is single or double,—to the word with which it is meant to rhyme. The literal translator, therefore, of any rhyming Latin poetry,—especially one that ventures, in translating such a master of rhyme as Adam of St. Victor, to keep intact both the number and the character of the original rhymes,—starts, handicapped, as it were, by the necessity of finding rhymes in numbers far greater than any English poetry, so far as I know, contains, and of a kind in which the English language is singularly poor. I venture to remind the critical reader of these facts, in the hope that they may serve to explain, if not to excuse, my shortcomings—which I am painfully aware of—in the matter of rhymes. I can only say that I have done my best to avoid even doubtful rhymes, and such as still disfigure my translations remain, because I have failed to find better ones to replace them.

I have thought it better on the whole,—chiefly in the interest of the translations,—to print the original Sequences and my own renderings of them upon opposite pages. I am aware that some, who will value the book simply for the sake of the Latin text, would have preferred having the translations printed at the end of each volume by themselves, but the poetry of Adam of St. Victor is of so peculiar a kind, that I think the majority of any readers I may be fortunate enough to secure, will like better to have the two placed as they are for the sake of ready comparison. The translations, if found to be tolerably correct, are naturally such an interpretation of the originals as to render long critical notes unnecessary, and such as there are I have remitted to the end of each volume, so as not to interfere with the appearance of the pages.

The notes themselves are principally confined to short accounts of the less known Saints commemorated by the poet, to Scripture references, and to explanations of the typology and symbolism—of both of which Adam is very fond—contained in the Sequences. I have gathered my information from the best, indeed the only, sources accessible to me in a country parsonage.

I should like to be able to thank by name *all* those who have aided me in many ways in my undertaking, but they are so many in number that I am compelled to content myself with a general expression of heart-felt gratitude in the case of the large majority of my kindly coadjutors. Some, however, I feel bound to mention more particularly.

To His Grace the Archbishop of Dublin,—the first "Victorine" scholar of the day,—I owe my grateful thanks for his kindness in helping me in not a few of the difficult and obscure passages to be found in the text of Adam; for his allowing me to use what he has written upon Adam, (a permission of which I have freely availed myself, as will be seen in the notes, &c.); and not least for his personal interest in the work of one who was a perfect stranger to him.

To Canon C. Page Eden, Vicar of Aberford, and to Dr.

Littledale I am equally and deeply indebted for assistance which must have involved no little time and labour even to such distinguished scholars as they are, and without which I should scarcely have dared to venture upon publication.

To Bishop Jenner, Dr. B. H. Kennedy, Canon of Ely, Regius Professor of Greek at Cambridge, W. S. Lilly, Esq., and to many others my thanks are due for help and interest in a work which I can only hope may not prove entirely unworthy of the kindness it has elicited towards myself during its progress.

I would only add how grateful I shall be to any of my readers who may be moved to point out defects, or to suggest improvements in what is still, I fear, very crude work. I shall grudge no additional time nor labour spent hereafter to make more worthy of their great original the interpretations I have essayed in these volumes of perhaps the noblest Mediæval Classic we possess.

D. S. W.

DARRINGTON,
1881.

CONTENTS OF THE FIRST VOLUME.

SEQUENCES FOR CHURCH SEASONS.

SEQUENCES FOR SAINTS' DAYS.

ADAM OF ST. VICTOR.

THE Abbey of St. Victor, from which the great Latin hymnologist takes his name, and which,—originally in the suburbs of Paris,—was later on absorbed into the city itself, as she enlarged her borders, was celebrated, especially in the twelfth century, as a school of theology.

Probably no other religious foundation could boast of such a brilliant *triad* of doctors of divinity, as the one that graced this Abbey during that century in the persons of Hugh of St. Victor, known to his generation as *Lingua Augustini;* his pupil, Richard of St. Victor, named *Alter Augustinus;* and Adam of St. Victor, the author of the Sequences[1] in these volumes, who, as will be apparent to the most cursory reader even, was deeply versed in the learning of the school to which he belonged. Beyond the fact, however, that they were monks of St. Victor, whose residence there—one or other of them—covered nearly the whole of the twelfth century, the accounts that we have left of them are exceedingly meagre and uncertain. They live for us now-a-days, very much as they must have lived, in the retirement of their monastic life, for their contemporaries, only in the books which they

[1] "SEQUENCE. The prolongation of the versicle of the Alleluia, instituted in order to give the deacon time to reach the pulpit to chant the Gospel. Gradually words were set to this cadence, and so came the Sequence. It is ascribed alike to S. Notker and Alcuin; the Sequences in rhythm are a development of later days. Originally the Sequence was called a *Prose*, because its early form was rhythmical prose."—*Orby Shipley's* "Glossary of Ecclesiastical Terms" (1872).

wrote,—of which, in all probability, we know more than their own generation did.

Hugh of St. Victor, the oldest of them, was by birth a Saxon; when he entered the Monastery of St. Victor we are not told. All we can glean about his chronology is that he died there either in A.D. 1139, or one of the two following years.

Richard of St. Victor, his pupil, and a native of Scotland, was more closely contemporaneous with Adam, the last and most brilliant of the three. There seems no reason to doubt that he was nearly of the same age as the latter, though his life was by no means so prolonged as that of Adam, if we are to accept the authority of an old MS., quoted by Gautier, as quoted by John of Toulouse; which describes the poet as being "Richardi Victorini contemporaneus, sed longe superstes."

Of Adam of St. Victor (so scanty are the materials for a biographical notice of him), we cannot certainly prove even the nationality. This much only seems to be certain, that he was a native either of England or Brittany. He is described generally in the MSS. of the period immediately succeeding his own as *Brito*, and the question remains, and must remain, unsettled, as to which of the two countries for which he is claimed as a native, that term refers. Of course in an Abbey where so many of the monks were evidently foreigners,—for neither Hugh nor Richard were Frenchmen,—it is possible that the great Mediæval poet was a fellow-countryman of ours; but Archbishop Trench—and it is a point upon which, as upon most others, we may safely defer to his better judgment—concludes, that "the fact that France was the main seat of Latin poetry in the twelfth century, and that all the most famous composers in this kind, as Hildebert, the two Bernards, Abelard, Marbod, Peter the Venerable, were Frenchmen, leaves it more likely that he, the first and foremost of all, was such as well!"

M. Gautier entertains no doubt,—and he has evidently been most indefatigable in his researches into all that relates personally, or poetically, to the object of them,—that, be he "Breton" or "Briton," Adam entered the religious foundation of St. Victor, as a young man, about A.D. 1130; after having, as Archbishop Trench says, "made his studies at Paris." Here he remained for the rest of his life, which was prolonged certainly to A.D. 1172, and probably, according to M. Gautier, to A.D. 1192. And here he wrote at various times, as the occasion called each forth, the series, and it is not a short one, of the Sequences on which his claim to literary honours mainly rests, and of which—however much English Churchmen must, in many points, decline to follow their doctrinal teaching — very few will fail to recognize the exceeding beauty, looked at as classical compositions merely, and fewer still, one would hope, to appreciate at their real value the exactness of their author's theology when dealing with the great Catholic doctrines which are common to almost the whole of Christendom, or the devotional spirit that breathes throughout his writings.

Lord Coleridge, the present Lord Chief Justice of England, in his preface to a re-publication by him in 1872 of the seventeenth century edition in English of "A Mirror of Monks," by *Lewis Blosius*, expresses so completely the sentiments by which I have been animated in dealing with the works of Adam of St. Victor, that I gladly and gratefully avail myself of his lordship's permission to quote a few sentences from it here, feeling sure that the reader will be glad to have an opinion on such a point from one whose opinion upon any point must carry great weight with it :—

"It is hardly necessary to say that I do not agree with every theological doctrine which Blosius assumes or inculcates in his book ; but I think the book in itself a good and beautiful book. I believe the writer of it to have been a holy man ; and I do not think it right, in spite of high authority to the contrary, to mutilate or adapt such works as these. To do so appears to me unmanly and unfair. It is as if we were afraid of the soundness of our convictions, and dared not look in the face the fact that good men of other times did not share them. Whereas it is part of Christian history that very good and saintly men have held opinions in religion which we now think mistaken; and it is a narrow and shallow judgment which holds such opinions to be inconsistent with true and vital Christianity. This book, to my mind, proves that they are nowise inconsistent: and I most earnestly hope that those who read it carefully will think so too."

The reader will have the opportunity of judging for himself as to the merits of the various Sequences as they come before him; but it may be well, perhaps, to say a few words as to their general character, and I know not that they can be said better than by one who has so thoroughly identified his name with Latin hymnology generally, and especially with that of the "Victorine School," as the present Archbishop (Trench) of Dublin:—

"Very different estimates have been formed of the merits of Adam of St. Victor's hymns. His most zealous admirers will hardly deny that he pushes too far, and plays overmuch with, his skill in the typical application of the Old Testament. So, too, they must own that sometimes he is unable to fuse his manifold learned allusion into the passion of his poetry. . . . Nor less must it be allowed that he is sometimes guilty of conceits, of plays upon words, not altogether worthy of the solemnity of his theme. Thus of one Martyr he says:—

'Sub securi stat securus;'

of another, Saint [Vincent] namely:—

'Dum torretur, non terretur;'

of the Blessed Virgin (for he did not escape, as it was not to be expected that he should, the exaggerations of his time):—

'O dulcis vena veniæ;'

of heaven:—

'O quam beata curia,
Quæ curæ prorsus nescia.'

Sometimes, too, he is overfond of displaying feats of skill in versification, or prodigally accumulating, or curiously interlacing his rhymes, that he may show his perfect mastery of the forms which he is using, and how little he is confined or trammelled by them.

"These faults it will be seen are indeed most of them but merits pushed into excess. And even accepting them as defects, his profound acquaintance with the whole circle of the theology of his time, and eminently with its exposition of Scripture,—the abundant and admirable use, with indeed the drawback already mentioned, which he makes of it, delivering as he thus does his poems from the merely *subjective* cast of those, beautiful as they are, of St. Bernard,—the exquisite art and variety with which for the most part his verse is managed and his rhymes disposed,—their rich melody multiplying and ever deepening at the close,—the strength which he often concentrates into a single line,[1] his skill in conducting a story,—and, most of all, the evident nearness of the things which he celebrates to his own heart of hearts,—all these, and other excellencies, render him, as far as my judgment goes, the foremost among the sacred Latin poets of the Middle Ages. He may have no single poem to vie with the austere grandeur of the *Dies Iræ*, nor yet with the tearful passion of the *Stabat Mater*, although concerning the last point there might well be a question; but then it must not be forgotten that these stand well-nigh alone in the names of

[1] Thus of a Roman governor, who, alternating flatteries with threats, is seeking to bribe St. Agnes from her allegiance to Christ by the offer of worldly dignities and honours:—

"Offert multa, spondet plura,
Periturus peritura."

their respective authors, while from his ample treasure-house I shall enrich this volume with a multitude of hymns, all of them of considerable, some of the very highest, merit. Indeed, were I disposed to name any one who might dispute the palm of sacred Latin poetry with him, it would not be one of these, but rather Hildebert, Archbishop of Tours."—*Sacred Latin Poetry*, pages 57-61.

It would be unnecessary for me, even were I able, which I am not, to add much to this eloquent and exhaustive summary of the merits, and defects as well, of this great poet. One point only, in what is characteristic of the author, is not touched upon, and that is his love of alliteration, carried at times perhaps to an excess like his play upon words,[1] but often used with striking effect.

The history of the Sequences in this work is a curious and a chequered one. As I said at the beginning of this notice, the Abbey of St. Victor, which in our poet's time was in the suburbs of Paris, was by the growth of the town afterwards included within its walls. There it remained undisturbed, and having Adam of St. Victor's poetry in its library, until the French Revolution, when, in common with all others, its religious foundation was dissolved, its inmates dispersed, and its precious MSS. removed, as it appeared afterwards, to the National Library in the Louvre. Some of Adam's Sequences had, during the centuries that the MSS. remained in the custody of the monks of the author's monastery, found their way into circulation, thirty-seven of them with his name attached to them, and a few others without any trace of the

[1] Take this instance from the Sequence "On the Passion of St. Quintin:"—

"Propter jugum Christi lene,
Premunt compes et catenæ
    Carcerali clausum cella;
Sed triumphat bonus bene
Universum genus pœnæ,
    Famem, frigus, et flagella."

writer. The thirty-seven were collected and published by Clichtoveus, "a Roman Catholic theologian of the first half of the sixteenth century," in his "Elucidatorium Ecclesiasticum," which passed through several editions from 1515 to 1556 at Paris, Basle, and Geneva. This work, which was written originally for the instruction of the clergy in the meaning of the various offices of the Church, according to Archbishop Trench, became invaluable to those who made Mediæval Hymnology their study, and was in fact the only collection of it on a large scale.

The remainder of the Sequences contained in these volumes, and which never saw the light (until they were discovered in the Louvre) from the date of the French Revolution up to the middle of this century, we owe to the persevering search after them which M. Gautier made about the latter date. Those published by him for the first time are forty-eight in number, and include some of the most striking of the whole collection. Of three the first line only survives, the remainder of the Sequences not having been found as yet; and it is more than probable that there may be more still written by Adam which cannot be assigned to him now, because it is a remarkable fact that, numerous as those hymns are of which he will henceforth have the credit, we do not possess a single Sequence of which he was professedly the author, upon so central a Christian truth as the Passion of our Lord, or one for Lent or Advent, which could hardly, one would imagine, have been the case always, seeing that the rest of the Christian year is so largely illustrated in his writings.

The collection, as M. Gautier gave it to the world, consisted of 106 Sequences, satisfactorily proved to have come from Adam of St. Victor's pen, viz., thirty-seven published and attributed to the author by Clichtoveus, two published by him without attribution, seventeen published in other collections without attribution, forty-seven published for the first time by Gautier, and the three mentioned above of which we have as yet only the first line. Besides these, however, there is the Epitaph of Adam, of which only the first ten lines were written by him, and eight Sequences doubtfully or wrongly attributed to him, but included in M. Gautier's volumes. All these, arranged as they were in the French edition, will be found in that now offered to the public.

The reader will, no doubt, be struck by the great variety of metres employed by the poet, not only in the Sequences, taken as a whole, but also in single Sequences. In some the metre changes several times during the course of them, and even single stanzas are constantly subjected to the same process. The effect is to give great variety to the hymns, generally and singly,—enabling the poet to introduce an amount of light and shade into his compositions which is impossible when one metre is rigidly adhered to throughout a poem. As all Adam's Sequences were originally set to music and used in the worship of his Abbey, a suggestion is perhaps allowable on my part, as to whether we might not now-a-days have some of the music in our choral services arranged upon a similar plan. As it is, we have nothing between the ordinary hymn in which the metre never changes, and for which, therefore, the same tune must be used throughout, and anthems, which, beautiful as they are, are far too elaborate and difficult for general use in our churches. The arrangement of these Mediæval hymns appears to me to combine the advantages, without the defects, of both hymns and anthems,—possessing as they do all the simplicity of the first without their sameness, and much of the variety of the last without their elaborateness. If we could vary the tunes in a single hymn, as is often done, as it is, in the *Te Deum* or the *Psalms* of the day, we should be enabled to increase not only the length of the hymns, which are now confined to four or six verses, but to add to their devotional effect as well by having both the metre *in* which, and the music *to* which the words are set somewhat more appropriate to the sentiments sought to be expressed than is always the case now.

But the metres of our poet are not only various in their arrangement, they, as a well-known labourer in the mine of Mediæval Hymnology, the Rev. Louis Coutier Biggs, says, "absolutely bristle with rhymes, ... These are distinguished," he adds "into—

"*Leonines*, rhyming the middle with the end of the line, thus :—

'Urit *ira* tua *dira*
O Traj*ane* inhum*ane*
   Propr*io* ex vit*io*
Sanctum Chr*isti* quum juss*isti*
Flagell*ari*, cruci*ari*
   Nim*io* supplic*io*.'

"*Caudate*, or tail-rhymes, are final rhymes following each other closely, as . . . . the hymn :—

'Lux illuxit Domini*ca*,
Lux insignis, lux uni*ca*,
Lux lucis et lætit*iæ*,
Lux immortalis glor*iæ*.

'Diem mundi condit*io*
Commendat ab init*io*,
Quam Christi resurrect*io*
Ditavit privileg*io*.'

"*Interlaqueate*, or interlaced rhymes, are such as we find in the Spenserian stanza, or in the poetry of Dante, *e.g.* :"—[1]

"Mundi renovatio
   Nova parit gaudia ;
Resurgenti Domino
   Conresurgunt omnia.
Elementa serviunt,
Et auctoris sentiunt
   Quanta sint sollemnia."

The critical reader, who may desire to follow up more closely than it is requisite to do in this notice of Adam of St. Victor, this part of the subject, will find an interesting

[1] "Monthly Packet" (New Series), vol. xi. page 544.

account of the metres employed by the poet in *Neale's* "Epistola de Sequentiis," published by *Daniel* at the beginning of his "Thesaurus Hymnologicus," vol. v.; as well as in *Gautier's* Introductory Essay on Adam and his Poetical and Prose Works, prefixed to the edition of 1858-59.

I will conclude this brief introductory notice of one who has been described by *Rambach* as the "Schiller of the Middle Ages;" by *Dom Gueranger* as "le plus grande poete du moyen age;" and by *Dr. Neale*—with almost pardonable exaggeration—as "to my mind the greatest Latin poet, not only of Mediæval, but of all, ages," with the passage that immediately follows that just quoted from the last-named writer in his Preface to "Mediæval Hymns," page x.

"It is a magnificent thing to pass along the far-stretching vista of hymns,—from the sublime self-containedness of S. Ambrose to the more fervid inspiration of S. Gregory, the exquisite typology of Venantius Fortunatus, the lovely painting of S. Peter Damiani, the crystal-like simplicity of S. Notker, the scriptural calm of Godescalcus, the subjective loveliness of S. Bernard, till all culminate in the full blaze of glory which surrounds Adam of S. Victor, the greatest of all. And though Thomas of Celano in one unapproachable sequence distanced him, and the author, whoever he were, of the *Verbum Dei Deo natum* once equalled him, what are we to think of the genius that could pour forth one hundred sequences, of which fifty at least are unequalled save by the *Dies Iræ?* . . . . Indeed, Adam is worth any pains and any study."

SEQUENCES FOR CHURCH SEASONS.

I.

NATIVITAS DOMINI.

POTESTATE, non natura,
Fit Creator creatura,
Reportetur ut factura
Factoris in gloria.
Prædicatus per prophetas,
Quem non capit locus, ætas,
Nostræ sortis intrat metas,
Non relinquens propria.

Castitatis in tenorem,
Plasma gignit plasmatorem,
Virgo parit amatorem,
Lactat patrem filia.
Argumentum genituræ
Hujus nescit jus naturæ;
Suæ legis fracto jure,
Stupet de potentia.

Cœlum terris inclinatur,
Homo-Deus adunatur;
Adunato famulatur

I.

CHRISTMAS.

THE Creator, not by nature
  But by might, becomes a creature,
That with glory the Creator
  May His creature once more crown.
Presaged in the prophets' pages,
He, Who of no place or age is,
Enters on our life's brief stages,
  Not relinquishing His own.

Virgin still, the creature giveth
Birth to Him through Whom she liveth;
Maiden's womb her spouse conceiveth;
  Daughter's breasts her father feed.
Nature's law no instance knoweth
Of such birth as this one showeth;
And, since it all law o'erthroweth,
  Nature trembles at the deed.

Heaven to earth hath condescended;
Man is with the Godhead blended,
And the Man-God is attended

Cœlestis familia.
Rex sacerdos consecratur
Generalis, quod monstratur
Cum pax terris nuntiatur
Et in altis gloria.

Causam quæris, modum rei:
Causa prius omnes rei,
Modus justum velle Dei,
Sed conditum gratia.
O quam dulce condimentum
Nobis mutans in pigmentum
Cum aceto fel cruentum
Degustante Messya!
O salubre sacramentum,
Quod nos ponit in jumentum
Plagis nostris dans unguentum
Ille de Samaria!

Ille alter Elyseus,
Reputatus homo reus,
Suscitavit homo-Deus
Sunamitis puerum.
Hic est gigas currens fortis,
Qui, destructo lege mortis,
Ad amœna primæ sortis
Ovem fert in humerum.

By celestial ministry.
That, as priest, is consecrated
Heaven's king, is demonstrated;
Peace on earth is promulgated,
Glory unto God on high!

Ask'st thou why? how? this beginneth.
Why? because mankind first sinneth;
How? God's just will then combineth
With His grace to break sin's thrall.
O how sweet their blended savour,
Changing into spiced wine's flavour,
When Christ tasted, man to favour,
Bitter vinegar and gall!
O dread mystery, soul-reviving!
When Samaria's son arriving
Sets, for wounds a balm contriving,
On His own beast those that fall!

He, Elisha's true successor,
God-man, counted a transgressor,
To the Shunamite, to bless her,
Hath restored her son again.
As a giant runs He joying,
Who, His shoulder's strength employing,
Bears His sheep, Death's law destroying,
Back to primal joys of men.

Vivit, regnat Deus-homo,
Trahens orco lapsum pomo;
Cœlo tractus gaudet homo
   Denum complens numerum.

Patris mater, meta vatum,
Ora Patrem, jube natum,
Nos ut ducat ad hunc statum
   Plenum pace, gloria,
      Quo refecti
      Visu Dei
   Cantemus Alleluia.
   —Amen dicant omnia!

As God-man He lives and reigneth,
And lost man from hell restraineth;
Man with joy heaven's realms obtaineth,
  Filling up its orders ten.

Heaven's Sire's mother, goal of sages!
Pray that Father through all ages,
Tell thy Son to point our stages .
  To where peace and glory reign;
    Till there, being
    Braced, God seeing,
  Lift we Alleluia's strain,
  Let creation say "Amen!"

II.

NATIVITAS DOMINI.

IN excelsis canitur
  Nato regi gloria,
Per quem terræ redditur
  Et cœlo concordia.

Jure dies colitur
  Christi natalitia,
Quo nascente nascitur
  Novæ legis gratia.

Mediator nobis datus
  In salutis pretium
Non naturæ, sed reatus
  Refugit consortium.

Non amittit claritatem
  Stella fundens radium
Nec Maria castitatem
  Pariendo filium.

II.

CHRISTMAS.

IN the highest, hark ! the strain,
  " Glory to the new-born King !
Who doth with Him peace, again
  Joining earth and heaven, bring !"

Honour thus is paid aright
  Unto this, Christ's natal morn ;
At Whose birth the grace so bright
  Of a new-made law is born.

The appointed Mediator,
  Our salvation's price to pay,
Not His share in human nature,
  But its misdeeds, puts away.

Not a whit less bright appearing,
  The life-giving star we see ;
Nor doth Mary by child-bearing
  Lose her spotless chastity.

Quid de monte lapis cæsus
Sine manu, nisi Jesus
  Qui de regum linea,
  Sine carnis opere,
  De carne puerperæ
  Processit virginea?

  Solitudo floreat
  Et desertum gaudeat!
  Virga Jesse floruit.
Radix virgam, virga florem,
Virgo profert Salvatorem,
  Sicut lex præcinuit.

Radix David typum gessit,
Virga matris quæ processit
  Ex regali semine;
Flos est Puer nobis natus,
Jure flori comparatus
  Præ mira dulcedine.

In præsepe reclinatur,
Cujus ortus celebratur
  Cœlesti præconio.
  Cœli cives jubilant,
  Dum pastores vigilant
  Sub noctis silentio.

What is this rock-stone so precious,
Quarried not by hand, but Jesus,
Scion of a line of kings,
Who, begot, without man's aid,
Of a pure yet pregnant maid,
From her fleshly nature springs?

Let the desert blossom forth;
Joy, waste places of the earth!
Jesse's rod doth flowers unfold.
Root it brancheth, branch it bloometh,
Virgin-born, a Saviour cometh,
As the law of old foretold.

David's self that root portended;
Mary is that branch, descended
From that seed of royal line:
He, the Son unto us given,
Is its flower, a flower from heaven,
Since its fragrance is divine.

He, Whose birth's due celebration
Forms the angels' proclamation,
In a manger-cradle lies;
Heavenly hosts therein delight,
Whilst the shepherds watch by night
'Neath the silence of the skies.

Cuncta laudes intonant
  Super partum Virginis ;
Lex et psalmi consonant
  Prophetarum paginis.

Angelorum et pastorum,
Stellæ simul et magorum
  Concordant indicia ;
Reges currunt Orientis
Ad præsepe vagientis,
  Gentium primordia.

Jesu, puer immortalis,
Ex æterno temporalis,
Nos ab hujus vitæ malis
  Tu potenter erue.
Tu, post vitam hanc mortalem,
Sive mortem hanc vitalem,
Vitam nobis immortalem
  Clementer restitue. Amen.

All things shouts of joy upraise
  For the Virgin's Son most high;
Him the law and psalms too praise
  With the page of prophecy.

Angels', shepherds', salutations,
Stars' and wise men's indications,
  In their object all agree:
Haste those Eastern kings where, crying,
In a crib a Babe is lying,
  Who the Gentile first-fruits be.

Infant Jesu, death-bound never!
For a time and yet for ever!
By Thy might mankind deliver
  From this life's adversity:
When this mortal life is ended,
From this living death ascended,
By Thy clemency befriended,
  Grant us deathless life with Thee! Amen.

III.

NATIVITAS DOMINI.

IN natale Salvatoris
Angelorum nostra choris
Succinat conditio:
Harmonia diversorum,
Sed in unum redactorum
Dulcis est connexio.

Felix dies hodiernus,
In quo Patri coæternus
Nascitur ex Virgine!
Felix dies et jocundus!
Illustrari gaudet mundus
Veri solis lumine.

Ne periret homo reus,
Redemptorem misit Deus,
Pater unigenitum;
Visitavit quos amavit
Nosque vitæ revocavit
Gratia, non meritum.

III.

CHRISTMAS.

SINCE a Saviour is born for us,
With the angels in glad chorus
Let our race unite to-day:
Sweetly sound such hymns uprising,
Different voices harmonizing
All their praises in one lay.

Happy day, when the Supernal,
With the Father co-eternal,
Of a Virgin comes to birth!
Day of joy and jubilation,
When the bright illumination
Of the true Sun lights glad earth!

God hath a Redeemer given,
His, the Father's, Son from heaven,
That the sinner should not die:
It is grace alone, not merit,
Gives us new life through the Spirit,
Visiting God's family.

Infinitus et immensus
Quem non capit ullus sensus
  Nec locorum spatia,
Ex æterno temporalis,
Ex immenso fit localis,
  Ut restauret omnia!

Non peccatum, sed peccati
Formam sumens, vetustati
  Nostræ se contemperat:
Immortalis se mortali,
Spiritalis corporali,
  Ut natura conferat.

Sic concurrunt in personæ
Singularis unione
  Verbum, caro, spiritus,
Ut natura non mutetur,
Nec persona geminetur,
  Sed sit una penitus.

Tantæ rei sacramentum
Latet hostem fraudulentum;
  Fallitur malitia.
Cæcus hostis non præsagit
Quod sub nube carnis agit
  Dei sapientia.

Infinite and in all places,
He, whom sense and earth's wide spaces
  Comprehend not nor contain,
Though eternal, time obeyeth,
And, though everywhere, here stayeth,
  All things to restore again!

He sin's form, without sin, weareth,
And, to be made like us, shareth
  Our worn-out existence here;
That the temporal and eternal,
That the spiritual and carnal,
  Natures might thus linked appear.

So the Word and Flesh and Spirit
Doth one Person thus inherit
  In mysterious union,
That no change its nature showeth,
Nor two-fold that Person groweth,
  But is altogether one.

This great mystery lies ever
Hidden from man's base deceiver,
  And at fault his malice is:
That the wisdom of the Godhead
'Neath the veil of flesh is shrouded
  Our blind enemy ne'er sees.

Hujus nodum sacramenti
Non subtilis argumenti
Solvit inquisitio.
Modum nosse non est meum;
Scio tamen posse Deum
Quod non capit ratio.

Quam subtile Dei consilium!
Quam sublime rei mysterium!
Virga florem,
Vellus rorem,
Virgo profert filium.

Nec pudorem læsit conceptio,
Nec virorem floris emissio;
Concipiens
Et pariens
Comparatur lilio.

O Maria, stella maris,
Post Deum spes singularis
Naufragantis sæculi,
Vide quam nos fraudulenter,
Quam nos vexant violenter
Tot et tales æmuli.

Per te virtus nobis detur,
Per te, mater, exturbetur
Dæmonum superbia;

This deep mystery's complication
No abstruse investigation
By induction can explain.
'Tis not mine to know its measure,
But I wot that God's good pleasure
Rules where reason cannot strain.

O how deep the counsel of God appears!
How sublime the mystery it declares!
Rod a flower,
Fleece a shower,
And a Son a Virgin bears.

Her conception hurt not her chastity,
Nor its blooming that ever verdant tree;
In conceiving
And birth-giving,
Lily-like, still pure is she!

Mary, star of ocean! giving
To this shipwrecked age we live in
After God its hope alone!
See what rival machinations,
And what fierce and dire temptations
Vex us sorely every one.

Virtue unto us be given,
And demonic pride be driven
Far away from us by Thee;

Tuæ proli nos commenda,
Ne nos brevis, sed tremenda
  Feriat sententia.

Jesu, noster salutaris,
Qui prudenter operaris
  Salutis mysterium,
His qui colunt hunc natalem
Da salutem temporalem,
  Da perhenne gaudium !

To thine offspring O commend us,
Lest His brief but most tremendous
  Sentence crush us utterly.

Jesu, Who art our salvation,
Who its wondrous operation
  With such wisdom watchest c'er!
Those, who keep this day, defending,
Here Thy help to them extending,
  Grant them joy for evermore!

IV.

NATIVITAS DOMINI.

LUX est orta gentibus,
In umbra sedentibus
Et mortis caligine.
Gaudet miser populus
Quia mundo parvulus
Nascitur de virgine.

Ut ascendat homo reus
Condescendit homo-Deus
Hominis miseriæ.
Quis non laudet et lætetur?
Quis non gaudens admiretur
Opus novæ gratiæ?

Quidnam jocundius,
Quidnam secretius
Tali mysterio?
O quam laudabilis!
O quam mirabilis
Dei dignatio!

IV.

CHRISTMAS.

FOR the Gentiles up hath sprung
Light, for those that sate among
Darkness and in death's deep gloom.
Joys a people all forlorn,
That on earth a Child is born
From a spotless maiden's womb.

Guilty man to raise to heaven,
Condescends the God-man even
To our nature's misery.
Who would not with joy be praising,
Songs of wondering gladness raising,
Grace-work of such novelty?

What is more full of bliss,
What is more fathomless,
Than such a mystery?
How worthy all our praise,
How unlike human ways,
Is God's humility!

Hujus nodum sacramenti
Non subtilis argumenti
Solvit inquisitio.
Modum nosse non est meum;
Scio tamen posse Deum
Quod non capit ratio.

Quam subtile Dei consilium!
Quam sublime rei mysterium!
Virga florem,
Vellus rorem,
Virgo profert filium.

Nec pudorem læsit conceptio,
Nec virorem floris emissio;
Concipiens
Et pariens
Comparatur lilio.

O Maria, stella maris,
Post Deum spes singularis
Naufragantis sæculi,
Vide quam nos fraudulenter,
Quam nos vexant violenter
Tot et tales æmuli.

This deep mystery's complication
No abstruse investigation
By induction can explain.
'Tis not mine to know its measure,
But I wot that God's good pleasure
Rules where reason cannot strain.

O how deep the counsel of God appears!
How sublime the mystery it declares!
Rod a flower,
Fleece a shower,
And a Son a Virgin bears!

Her conception hurt not her chastity,
Nor its blooming that ever verdant tree;
In conceiving
And birth-giving,
Lily-like, still pure is she!

Mary, star of ocean! giving
To this shipwrecked age we live in
After God its hope alone!
See what rival machinations,
And what fierce and dire temptations
Vex us sorely every one.

Per te virtus nobis detur,
Per te, mater, exturbetur
  Dæmonum superbia ;
Tuæ proli nos commenda,
Ne nos brevis, sed tremenda
  Feriat sententia.

Virtue unto us be given,
And demonic pride be driven
  Far away from us by Thee;
To thine offspring O commend us,
Lest His brief but most tremendous
  Sentence crush us utterly.

V.

NATIVITAS DOMINI.

JUBILEMUS Salvatori
Quem cœlestes laudant chori
Concordi lætitia;
Pax de cœlo nuntiatur,
Terra cœlo fœderatur,
Angelis Ecclesia.

Verbum carni counitum,
Sicut erat præfinitum,
Sine carnis copula
Virgo parit, Dei templum,
Nec exemplar, nec exemplum
Per tot habens sæcula.

Res est nova, res insignis,
Quod in rubo rubet ignis
Nec rubum attaminat:
Cœli rorant, nubes pluunt,
Montes stillant, colles fluunt,
Radix Jesse germinat.

V.

CHRISTMAS.

SONGS of joy let us be raising
To that Saviour now, in praising
Whom with us heaven's choirs delight;
News of peace from heaven is brought us,
Heaven is leagued with earth about us,
And the Church with angels bright.

God the Word, with our flesh blended,
As beforehand was intended,
She, who never knew a man,
Virgin, bears, God's temple hallowed,
Following none, by no one followed,
Ever since the world began.

That a bush with red fire gloweth,
Yet the fire no harm there doeth,
Is a new and wondrous thing:
Heaven drops dew, the clouds rain fountains,
Melt the hills and drip the mountains,
Jesse's root doth upward spring.

De radice flos ascendit
Quem prophetæ præostendit
  Evidens oraculum:
Radix Jesse regem David,
Virga matrem designavit
  Virginem, flos parvulum.

Ut ascendat homo reus,
Condescendit homo-Deus
  Hominis miseriæ.
Quis non laudet et lætetur?
Quis non gaudens admiretur
  Opus novæ gratiæ?

  Quidnam jocundius,
  Quidnam secretius
    Tali mysterio?
  O quam mirabilis!
  O quam laudabilis
    Dei dignatio!

Mira floris pulchritudo
Quem commendat plenitudo
  Septiformis gratiæ.
Recreemur in hoc flore
Qui nos gustu, nos odore,
  Nos invitat specie.

From that root a flower upgroweth,
As the prophet plainly showeth
  In his prophecy of yore :
David as that root appeareth,
As the rod the maid that beareth,
  As its flower the Child she bore.

Guilty man to raise to heaven,
Condescends the God-man even
  To our nature's misery.
Who would not with joy be praising,
Songs of wondering gladness raising,
  Grace-work of such novelty?

What is more full of bliss,
What is more fathomless,
  Than such a mystery?
How worthy all our praise,
How unlike human ways,
  Our God's humility!

Wondrous beauty hath the flower,
That rich grace's sevenfold dower
  Hath commended to our care.
Let us in this flower delight us,
Which doth both by taste invite us,
  And by scent and semblance rare.

Jesu, puer immortalis,
Tuus nobis hic natalis
  Pacem det et gaudia;
Flos et fructus virginalis,
Cujus odor est vitalis,
  Tibi laus et gloria!

Jesu, Infant death-defying!
May Thy birthday be supplying
  Peace to us and joys divine:
Flower and fruit of spotless maiden,
With immortal fragrance laden!
  Glory and great praise be Thine!

VI.

NATIVITAS DOMINI.

NATO nobis Salvatore
Celebremus cum honore
Diem natalitium,
Nobis datus, nobis natus,
Et nobiscum conversatus
Lux et salus gentium.

Eva prius interemit,
Sed Salvator nos redemit
Carnis suæ merito.
Prima parens nobis luctum,
Sed Maria vitæ fructum
Protulit cum gaudio.

Negligentes non neglexit,
Sed ex alto nos prospexit
Pater mittens Filium;
Præsens mundo, sed absconsus,
De secreto tanquam sponsus
Prodiit in publicum.

VI.

CHRISTMAS.

SINCE a Saviour is born for us,
Let us, honouring Him, in chorus
Celebrate His natal day,
To us given, for us even
Born, a man 'mongst men, from heaven,
As all nations' light and stay.

Death we first from Eve inherit,
But redemption through the merit
Of the Saviour's fleshly birth.
Sorrow our first parent bore us,
But the fruit, which shall restore us,
Mary with great joy brought forth.

Caring for the careless even,
God the Father looked from heaven,
Sending down His Son on earth:
In the world, yet from it hidden,
As a bridegroom, when thus bidden,
From His chamber Christ came forth.

Gigas velox, gigas fortis,
Gigas nostræ victor mortis,
    Accinctus potentia,
Ad currendam venit viam,
Complens in se prophetiam
    Et legis mysteria.

Jesu, nostra salutaris
Medicina, singularis
    Nostra pax et gloria,
Quia servis redimendis
Tam decenter condescendis,
    Te collaudant omnia!

Giant swift and giant glorious,
Giant o'er our death victorious,
Girt with power and majesty,
Came to run His course, fulfilling
All that seers had been foretelling,
And the Law's whole mystery.

Jesu, our salvation-giving
Balm, Who only on all living
Peace and glory canst bestow!
Since, Thy servants to deliver,
Thou dost stoop in love, for ever
All things join Thy praise to show!

VII.

NATIVITAS DOMINI.

SPLENDOR Patris et figura
Se conformans homini.
Potestate, non natura,
Partum dedit Virgini.

Adam vetus,
Tandem lætus,
Novum promat canticum;
Fugitivus
Et captivus
Prodeat in publicum!

Eva luctum,
Vitæ fructum
Virgo gaudens edidit;
Nec sigillum
Propter illum
Castitatis perdidit.

VII.

CHRISTMAS.

FASHIONED as a human creature,
Christ, His Father's image clear,
By His power, and not by nature,
Caused a Virgin's womb to bear.

No more grieving,
New songs weaving,
Let old Adam sing for mirth !
Exiles flying !
Captives lying
Prison-bound ! come boldly forth !

Eve bore sadness,
But with gladness
Fruit of life a Virgin bears ;
While unbroken
Still the token
Of her chastity appears.

Si crystallus sit humecta
Atque soli sit objecta,
Scintillat igniculum :
Nec crystallus rumpitur,
Nec in partu solvitur
Pudoris signaculum.

Super tali genitura
Stupet usus et natura,
Deficitque ratio ;
Res est ineffabilis
Tam pia, tam humilis
Christi generatio.

Frondem, florem, nucem sicca
Virga profert, et pudica
Virgo Dei Filium.
Fert cœlestem vellus rorem,
Creatura Creatorem,
Creaturæ pretium.

Frondis, floris, nucis, roris
Pietati Salvatoris
Congruunt mysteria.
Frons est Christus protegendo,
Flos dulcore, nux pascendo,
Ros cœlesti gratia.

If a crystal that is wetted
To the sun's rays be submitted,
    It emits a little spark;
    Neither doth the crystal break,
    Neither doth this child-birth take
    From the maid her maiden-mark.

Such begetting of a creature
Strikes experience dumb, and nature;
    Reason too fails utterly;
    Words could ne'er be found to show
    Birth so loving, birth so low,
    As at Christ's nativity.

Leaf, flower, nut, a dry rod beareth,
And a maiden pure prepareth
    To produce God's Son Most High.
From a fleece heaven's dew-shower springeth;
She, He made, her Maker bringeth
    Forth, what He had made to buy.

In the flower, leaf, nut, and shower
Mystic emblems of the power
    Of the Saviour's love are met.
Leaf Christ is—by shelter spreading;
Flower—by sweetness; *nut*—by feeding;
    Dew—by grace with heaven's dew wet.

Cur, quod virgo peperit,
    Est Judæis scandalum,
Cum virga produxerit
    Sicca sic amygdalum?

Contemplemur adhuc nucem;
Nam prolata nux in lucem
    Lucis est mysterium.
Trinam gerens unionem,
Tria confert: unctionem,
    Lumen et edulium.

Nux est Christus, cortex nucis
Circa carnem pœna crucis,
    Testa corpus osseum.
    Carne tecta Deitas
    Et Christi suavitas
    Signatur per nucleum.

Lux est cæcis, et unguentum
Christus ægris, et fomentum
    Piis animalibus.
O quam dulce sacramentum!
Fœnum carnis in frumentum
    Convertit fidelibus.

Why should it offend the Jews,
That a virgin bore a son,
When a rod could thus produce
Almonds, though a sapless one?

On the nut still let us ponder;
For, if a full light brought under,
'Tis the mystic type of light.
As it three in one appeareth,
So three gifts too it conferreth;
Unction, food, effulgence bright.

Christ the *nut*,—its *hull* His passion,
Closing round His human fashion,—
And His bony frame its *shell*,—
The incarnate Deity
And Christ's tender sympathy
In the *kernel* mark ye well.

Christ is light to those not seeing,
Balm, the sick from sickness freeing,
And His loving creatures' food.
O how sweet a rite! He taketh
Grass—*our flesh*—and thereof maketh
Grain for those who trust in God.

Quos sub umbra sacramenti,
Jesu, pascis in præsenti,
Tuo vultu satia.
Splendor Patri coæterne,
Nos hinc transfer ad paternæ
Claritatis gaudia. Amen.

Those, whose food Thou now providest,
Jesu! as 'neath rites Thou hidest,
With Thy presencc satiate!
Thou, the Father's Co-eternal
Brightness! us to joys supernal
In His glory hence translate! Amen.

VIII.

DIES CIRCUMCISIONIS.

HAC die festa concinat multimoda camœna,
Collaudans cœli Dominum cum dulci cantilena.

Per hæc enim solempnia sunt cuncta renovata,
Humano quoque generi est venia donata.

Invenit drachma mulier ; accenditur lucerna,
In carne dum comparuit mens Deo coæterna.

Dum cadit secus Jericho vir Hierosolomita,
Samaritanus affuit quo lapso datur vita.

Perduxit hunc in stabulum clementia divina,
Vinum permiscens oleo suavi medicina.

VIII.

THE CIRCUMCISION OF CHRIST.

THIS festal day our Muse should be a varied song upraising,
In strains of sweetest melody the Lord of heaven praising.

For all things by this festival have been renewed from heaven,
And pardon to the human race for all their misdeeds given.

The woman finds her silver piece; her candle she hath lighted,
What time to flesh the mind, with God co-equal, is united.

When from Jerusalem the man nigh Jericho is lying,
The good Samaritan comes by and rescues him from dying.

By clemency divine he is into the inn attended,
Whilst wine and oil, as remedy to soothe his pain, are blended.

Curantis ægri vulnera sunt dulcia fomenta,
Dum cunctis pœnitentia fuit reis inventa.

Bini dati denarii sunt duo Testamenta
Dum Christus, finis utriusque, complet sacramenta.

En tellus rore germinat nec patet madefacta,
Dum virgo Deum parturit, et mater est intacta.

In tenebris exortus est Puer, lux sempiterna;
Octava circumcisus est hac die hodierna.

Hæc ab antiquis patribus dies fuit prævisa
Dum se prolemque Domino dant carne circumcisa.

Hac die circumcisio fiebat sub figura
Octava, qua salvabitur humana creatura.

Sweet are the balms of Him, who gives to sick men's wounds their healing,
The way of penitence for all their sinfulness revealing.

Of the two Testaments the gift of the two pennies telleth,
Since Jesus Christ, the end of both, their mysteries fulfilleth.

Lo! now the earth buds forth with dew and yet abideth rainless,
Whilst bears a maid our God Himself, and is a mother stainless.

In darkness was the Infant born, Who light eternal giveth;
And circumcision on this day, the eighth day, He receiveth.

This day the Patriarchs of old foresaw in clear prevision,
Who gave themselves and progeny to God by circumcision.

That circumcision was performed this eighth day in a figure,
Which shall a human creature save from God's most righteous rigour.

Ergo nos circumcidamus, non carnis preputia,
Sed a nobis abscidamus sordes et vitia.

Ut mundati mente, carne, capiamus præmia,
Quæ octava confert ætas merenti cœlestia.

Eya, die ista,
Omnis organista
Cantor et psalmista
    Intonet,
    Consonet
Cum cytharista. Amen.

Ourselves, and not our foreskins, then let us be circumcising,
And cut away the lust and sin for aye within us rising.

That, cleansed in heart and flesh, to us those prizes may be given,
Which the eighth age confers on him deserving joy in heaven.

Come ye then to-day here,
Every organ-player,
Singer and psalm-sayer!
Lift your praise,
And upraise,
Minstrel! your lay here! Amen.

IX.

PASCHA.

ECCE dies celebris!
Lux succedit tenebris,
Morti resurrectio.
Lætis cedant tristia,
Cum sit major gloria
Quam prima confusio;
Umbram fugat veritas,
Vetustatem novitas,
Luctum consolatio.

Pascha novum colite;
Quod præit in capite,
Membra sperent singula.
Pascha novum Christus est,
Qui pro nobis passus est,
Agnus sine macula.

Hosti qui nos circuit
Prædam Christus eruit:
Quod Samson præcinuit,
Dum leonem lacerat.

IX.

EASTER.

HAIL, great day of wondrous deeds!
Light to deepest gloom succeeds,
And to death new risen life.
Joy all sorrow triumphs o'er,
For the glory now is more
Than the former mingled strife;
Truth the shadow puts to flight,
What is new the old and trite,
Consolation tears and grief.

Hail to our new Passover;
What the Head did first secure
May each member hope to gain.
Our new Passover is Christ,
Who for us was sacrificed,
As a Lamb devoid of stain.

From the foe about our way
Christ delivers now the prey,
E'en as Samson once did say,
When the lion he slew of yore.

David, fortis viribus,
A leonis unguibus
Et ab ursi faucibus
Gregem patris liberat.

Qui in morte plures stravit,
Samson, Christum figuravit,
Cujus mors victoria.
Samson dictus *Sol eorum* :
Christus lux est electorum,
Quos illustrat gratia.

Jam de Crucis sacro vecte
Botrus fluit in dilectæ
Penetral ecclesiæ.
Jam, calcato torculari,
Musto gaudent ebriari
Gentium primitiæ.

Saccus scissus et pertusus
In regales transit usus :
Saccus fit soccus gratiæ,
Caro victrix miseriæ.

Quia regem peremerunt,
Dei regnum perdiderunt :
Sed non deletur penitus
Cain, in signum positus.

David, strong in his good cause,
Rescues from the lion's claws
And the bear's devouring jaws,
All his father's flock once more.

Samson slew the most when dying,
Jesus Christ thus typifying,
Death to Whom was victory.
Samson's name " Their Sun " declareth ;
As His saints' light Christ appeareth,
Whom He shines on graciously.

From the Cross's holy transom
Flows the grapes' divinest ransom
To the well-loved Church's shrine :
Round the trodden wine-press thronging,
Gentile first-fruits drink, with longing,
Draughts of new and gladdening wine.

Sackcloth, worn to rags and riven,
Is to royal uses given :
With sackcloth shod, see ! peace doth go ;
The flesh hath triumphed over woe.

They are from God's kingdom driven,
Who to death its king have given :
Cain hath not wholly perished yet,
But for a warning sign is set.

Reprobatus et abjectus
Lapis iste, nunc electus,
In tropæum stat erectus,
    Et in caput anguli.
Culpam delens, non naturam,
Novam creat creaturam,
Tenens in se ligaturam
    Utriusque populi.

    Capiti sit gloria,
Membrisque concordia! Amen.

Though condemned once and rejected
Was this stone, it stands erected
For a trophy now, selected
    As the chiefest corner-stone.
Sin, not nature, He rebateth,
A new creature He createth,
And Himself incorporateth
    Jews and Gentiles into one.

    To the Head all glory be,
'Mongst the members unity ! Amen.

X.

PASCHA.

LUX illuxit Dominica,
Lux insignis, lux unica,
Lux lucis et lætitiæ,
Lux immortalis gloriæ.

Diem mundi conditio
Commendat ab initio,
Quam Christi resurrectio
Ditavit privilegio.

In spe perennis gaudii,
Lucis exultent filii;
Vindicent membra meritis
Conformitatem capitis!

Solemnis est celebritas
Et vota sunt solemnia;
Primæ diei dignitas
Prima requirit gaudia.

X.

EASTER.

THE Lord's own day hath poured its rays,
That glorious light, the day of days;
The light of light and joy, the day
Whose glory passeth not away.

This day the world's foundations laid
Distinguish, since the world was made;
On which Christ's rising from the dead
Hath new peculiar glory shed.

Ye sons of light! with lifted voice
In hope of endless joys rejoice;
And by good deeds, ye members! see
That like unto your Head ye be!

A holy feast this day displays,
And prayers as holy it desires;
The glory of the first of days
The first-fruits of our joy requires.

Solemnitatum gloria,
Paschalis est victoria,
Sub multis ænigmatibus
Prius promissa patribus.

Jam scisso velo patuit
Quod vetus lex præcinuit;
Figuram res exterminat,
Et umbram lux illuminat.

Quid agnus sine macula,
Quid hædus typi gesserit,
Nostra purgans piacula,
Messias nobis aperit.

Per mortem nos indebitam
Solvit a morte debita;
Prædam captans illicitam
Præda privatur licita.

Carnis delet opprobria
Caro peccati nescia;
Die reflorens tertia
Corda confirmat dubia.

The feast of Easter's victory
The glory of all feasts must be,
'Neath many a mystic type foretold
In promise to our sires of old.

Now, rent the veil, is that well known
In the old law obscurely shown;
Fulfilment types obliterates,
And shadows light illuminates.

From what the lamb without a spot,
From what the scapegoat, typified,
Purging from us guilt's sinful blot,
Messias draws the veil aside.

By death deserved not doth He pay
From death deserved to set us free;
Death, seizing the unlawful prey,
Loses what was his lawfully.

That flesh, which knows nor guilt nor stain,
Destroys our guilt, the flesh's bane;
And, springing the third day again,
Doth doubting hearts' full faith maintain.

O mors Christi mirifica,
Tu Christo nos vivifica!
Mors morti non obnoxia,
Da nobis vitæ præmia!

O death of Christ, most wondrous death!
Be thou in Christ our life and breath!
O death, that bows no death beneath!
Grant thou to us life's glory-wreath!

XI.

PASCHA.

SALVE, dies dierum gloria,
Dies felix, Christi victoria,
Dies digna jugi lætitia,
Dies prima!
Lux divina cæcis irradiat,
In qua Christus infernum spoliat,
Mortem vincit et reconciliat
Summis ima.

Sempiterni Regis sententia
Sub peccato conclusit omnia,
Ut infirmis superna gratia
Subveniret.
Dei virtus et sapientia
Temperavit iram clementia
Cum jam mundus in præcipitia
Totus iret.

Insultabat nostræ miseriæ,
Vetus hostis, auctor malitiæ,
Quia nulla spes erat veniæ
De peccatis;

XI.

EASTER.

HAIL, day, the glory of all days, to thee!
Thrice happy day, Christ's day of victory!
The first day! day most fit continually
Our joy to show!
This day divine illuminates blind eyes,
Upon which Christ of hell's dark realms makes prize,
O'ercometh death and joins in one the skies
And earth below.

The judgment of the everlasting King
Hath under sin concluded everything,
That heavenly grace the weak and wavering
Might come to aid.
God's goodness and His wisdom from on high
His wrath hath tempered with His clemency,
Now when all earth was being rapidly
In ruin laid.

The father of all lies, man's ancient foe,
Was trampling on us in our bitter woe,
Because no hope of pardon here below
For sin was left;

Desperante mundo remedium,
Dum tenerent cuncta silentium,
Deus Pater emisit Filium
Desperatis.

Prædo vorax, monstrum tartareum,
Carnem videns, nec cavens laqueum,
In latentem ruens aculeum
Aduncatur;
Dignitatis primæ conditio
Reformatur nobis in Filio
Cujus nova nos resurrectio
Consolatur.

Resurrexit liber ab inferis
Restaurator humani generis,
Ovem suam reportans humeris
Ad superna.
Angelorum pax fit et hominum;
Plenitudo succrescit ordinum:
Triumphantem laus decet Dominum,
Laus æterna!

Harmoniæ cœlestis patriæ
Vox concordet matris ecclesiæ;
Alleluia frequentet hodie
Plebs fidelis.

When thus the earth despaired of cure for sin,
And silence reigned o'er it and all therein,
Forth God the Father sent His Son to men
Of hope bereft.

The insatiate robber, monster hell did bear,
Seeing the bait, but heedless of the snare,
Rushing upon the hook's point hidden there,
On it is caught;
The dignity of man, as first begun,
Is now re-fashioned for us in the Son,
By Whose new resurrection to each one
Comfort is brought.

Free hath He risen from depths of hell below,
Who hath the human race re-fashioned so,
And, on His shoulder borne, His sheep He now
To heaven doth raise.
'Twixt men and angels is there perfect peace;
The ranks of heaven now swell to full increase;
Praise to the Lord Who maketh wars to cease,
Eternal praise!

O let the voice of Mother-Church agree
With heaven, our fatherland's, bright harmony,
And alleluias from the faithful be
Countless to-day!

Triumphato mortis imperio,
Triumphali fruamur gaudio:
In terra pax et jubilatio
Sit in cœlis! Amen.

The power of death o'ercome effectually,
Let us enjoy the joys of victory:
On earth be peace and jubilee on high
    In heaven for aye! Amen.

XII.

PASCHA.

SEXTA passus feria
Die Christus tertia
Resurrexit;
Surgens cum victoria,
Collocat in gloria
Quos dilexit.

Pro fideli populo
Crucis in patibulo
Immolatur;
Clauditur in tumulo,
Tandem in diluculo
Suscitatur.

Christi crux et passio
Nobis est præsidio,
Si credamus;
Christi resurrectio
Facit ut a vitio
Resurgamus.

XII.

EASTER.

CHRIST, upon the Friday slain,
On the Sunday once again
Rose victorious,
And those, whom He sought in love,
Gathers round Himself above,
Ever glorious.

For His faithful people He,
Offered on the Cross's tree,
Death sustaineth:
To the tomb's enclosure borne,
Life once more at early morn
He regaineth.

Christ's protection we receive
Through His Cross, if we believe,
And His Passion;
While His rising for our sakes
Possible our rising makes
From transgression.

Hostia sufficiens
Christus fuit moriens
Pro peccato ;
Sanguinis effusio
Abluit nos, impio
Triumphato.

Morte sua simplici
Nostræ morti duplici
Fert medelam ;
Vitæ pandit aditum,
Nostrum sanat genitum
Et querelam.

Leo fortis hodie
Dat signum potentiæ
Resurgendo,
Principem nequitiæ
Per arma justitiæ
Devincendo.

Diem istam Dominus
Fecit, in qua facinus
Mundi lavit,
In qua mors occiditur,
In qua vita redditur,
Hostis ruit.

A sufficient sacrifice
Jesus by His death supplies
    For all evil:
Through His blood, shed, cleansed are we,
And thus gain the victory
    O'er the devil.

He, by dying once for all,
Freedom from death's double thrall
    For us gaining,
Opens wide the gate of life,
Thereby healing all our grief
    And complaining.

He, the lion strong, to-day
Rising, of his powerful sway
    Token showeth;
For iniquity's fell lord,
He with righteousness's sword
    Overthroweth.

'Tis the Lord's own day, wherein
All the world, made clean from sin,
    He recalleth,
Whereon, death's self being slain,
And our life restored again,
    Satan falleth.

Geminatum igitur
Alleluya canitur
  Corde puro,
Quia culpa tollitur
Et vita promittitur
  In futuro.

In hoc mundi vespere
Fac tuos resurgere,
  Jesu Christe;
Salutaris omnibus
Sit tuis fidelibus
  Dies iste! Amen.

Therefore from pure hearts once more
Double alleluias soar
    Up to heaven;
Since away man's guilt is ta'en,
And that he shall live again
    Promise given.

Jesu Christ! make Thou Thine own
Rise before the sun goes down
    O'er creation;
May this day to all who bear
True allegiance to Thee here,
    Bring salvation! Amen.

XIII.

PASCHA.

MUNDI renovatio
Nova parit gaudia;
Resurgenti Domino
Conresurgunt omnia.
Elementa serviunt,
Et auctoris sentiunt
Quanta sint sollemnia.

Ignis volat mobilis,
Et aer volubilis,
Fluit aqua labilis,
Terra manet stabilis:
Alta petunt levia,
Centrum tenent gravia,
Renovantur omnia.

Cœlum fit serenius,
Et mare tranquillius;
Spirat aura levius,
Vallis nostra floruit.

XIII.

EASTER.

SPRING'S renewal of earth's plain
  New-born joys to man supplies;
When the Lord doth rise again,
  With Him also all things rise:
Elements upon Him wait,
Feeling, as their source, how great
  Should be His solemnities.

Fires their swift flames upward throw,
Lightly the air-eddies blow,
Running waters onward flow,
Earth remains unmoved below:
Light things soar above the plain,
Heavy things their place retain,
All things are renewed again.

Heights of heaven serener be,
And more tranquil grows the sea;
Breathes the air more buoyantly,
  And our vale fresh verdure shows;

Revirescunt arida,
Recalescunt frigida
Postquam ver intepuit.

Gelu mortis solvitur,
Princeps mundi tollitur,
Et ejus destruitur
In nobis imperium;
Dum tenere voluit
In quo nihil habuit,
Jus amisit proprium.

Vita mortem superat;
Homo jam recuperat
Quod prius amiserat
Paradisi gaudium:
Viam præbat facilem,
Cherubim versatilem
Amovendo gladium.

Christus cœlos reserat
Et captivos liberat
Quos culpa ligaverat
Sub mortis interitu.
Pro tanta victoria
Patri, Proli gloria
Sit cum Sancto Spiritu! Amen.

What is dry once more revives,
What is cold new heat receives,
  When with warmth the springtide glows.

Icy death dissolves to-day;
This world's prince is borne away,
And o'er us his hateful sway
  Is destroyed for evermore:
Since he in possession sought
Him in whom he had not aught,
  He hath lost his ancient power.

Death by life is triumphed o'er;
Man recovers now once more
All the bliss, which, lost of yore,
  Paradise's joys afford:
Easy hath the way there proved,
Since the cherubim removed
  Thence his ever-turning sword.

Christ re-opens heaven again,
Loosing every captive's chain,
Bound to undergo death's pain
  For his foul iniquity.
Glory for such victory won
To the Father and the Son
  With the Holy Spirit be! Amen.

XIV.

PASCHA.

ZYMA vetus expurgetur
Ut sincere celebretur
Nova resurrectio :
Hæc est dies nostræ spei,
Hujus mira vis diei
Legis testimonio.

Hæc Ægyptum spoliavit
Et Hebræos liberavit
De fornace ferrea :
His in arcto constitutis
Opus erat servitutis
Lutum, later, palea.

Jam Divina laus virtutis,
Jam triumphi, jam salutis
Vox erumpet libera !
Hæc est dies quam fecit Dominus,
Dies nostri doloris terminus,
Dies salutifera !

XIV.

EASTER.

PURGE away the former leaven,
That true thanks may now be given
On the day which saw Christ rise!
Hope to us this great day yieldeth;
Mighty is the power it wieldeth,
As the Law's word testifies.

Egypt's sons this day were plundered;
Israel's tribes, their fetters sundered,
From the kilns were freed to-day;
Servile was the occupation
Of this bound and captive nation,
Making bricks of straw and clay.

Of God's goodness let laudation,
Songs of triumph and salvation,
Burst forth now in accents clear:
This is the day the Lord Himself hath made,
The day our sorrows all to rest are laid,
And which brings salvation near.

Lex est umbra futurorum,
Christus, finis promissorum,
Qui consummat omnia:
Christi sanguis igneam
Hebetavit romphæam,
Amota custodia.

Puer nostri forma risus,
Pro quo vervex est occisus,
Vitæ signat gaudium.
Joseph exit de cisterna:
Christus redit ad superna,
Post mortis supplicium.

Hic dracones Pharaonis
Draco vorat, a draconis
Immunis malitia:
Quos ignitus vulnerat,
Hos serpentis liberat
Ænei præsentia.

Anguem forat in maxilla
Christi hamus et armilla:
In cavernam reguli
Manum mittit ablactatus,
Et sic fugit exturbatus
Vetus hospes sæculi.

Things to come the Law's type veileth;
Christ the promises fulfilleth,
Who doth all things consummate;
Christ's own blood, for us outpoured,
Making blunt the flaming sword,
Drives the warders from the gate.

Life's joy he, that lad, implieth,
Who our laughter typifieth,
In whose stead the ram was slain:
Joseph from the pit ascendeth,
Back to heaven His way Christ wendeth,
Having died His death of pain.

'Tis this serpent that devoureth
Pharaoh's serpents, and o'erpowereth,
Scatheless, the old serpent's spite.
He provideth an escape,
In a brazen serpent's shape,
From the fiery serpent's bite.

Christ the hook and thorn appeareth,
Which the serpent's jaw-bone teareth:
On the cockatrice's den
When His hand this weaned child layeth,
Driven off, no longer stayeth
That old dweller amongst men.

Irrisores Elisæi,
Dum conscendit domum Dei,
   Zelum calvi sentiunt:
   David arreptitius,
   Hircus emissarius
   Et passer effugiunt.

In maxilla mille sternit,
Et de tribu sua spernit
   Samson matrimonium:
Samson Gazæ seras pandit,
Et asportans portas scandit
   Montis supercilium.

Sic de Juda leo fortis,
Fractis portis diræ mortis,
   Die surgit tertia;
Rugiente voce patris
Ad supernæ sinum matris
   Tot revexit spolia.

Cetus Jonam fugitivum,
Veri Jonæ signativum,
Post tres dies reddit vivum
   De ventris angustia.

Mocking children, insults throwing
At the seer to Beth-el going,
  Feel the bald-head's righteous wrath:
David, by feigned madness stirred,
The scapegoat, the "living bird,"
  From the haunts of men flee forth.

Samson with a jaw-bone slayeth
Thousands, and contempt displayeth
  For a wife from 'mongst his own:
Samson Gaza's bolts unfastens,
And, its gates uplifting, hastens
  With them to the mountain's crown.

Judah's lion by this token
Boldly, death's dread portals broken,
  Rises the third day once more:
Back to Heaven rich fruits of daring
To our mother's bosom bearing,
  When He hears the Father's roar.

Jonah, from his duty flying,
Three days in her belly lying,
Our true Jonah typifying,
  Doth the whale restore alive.

Botrus Cypri reflorescit,
Dilatatur et excrescit;
Synagogæ flos marcescit,
  Et floret ecclesia.

Mors et vita conflixere,
Resurrexit Christus vere,
Et cum Christo surrexere
  Multi testes gloriæ.
Mane novum, mane lætum
Vespertinum tergat fletum:
Quia vita vicit letum,
  Tempus est lætitiæ.

Jesu victor, Jesu vita,
Jesu vitæ via trita,
Cujus morte mors sopita,
Ad Paschalem nos invita
  Mensam cum fiducia.
Vive panis, vivax unda,
Vera vitis et fecunda,
Tu nos pasce, tu nos munda,
Ut a morte nos secunda
  Tua salvet gratia. Amen.

Clustered camphire fresh life showeth,
Spreads abroad and larger groweth :
Blight alone the Law's bud knoweth,
  And the Church doth bloom and thrive.

Death and life's long strife is ended !
Christ hath risen indeed, attended
By a witness crowd, ascended
  With Him, who His glory show.
Morning new, morn gladness reaping !
Wipe away our eve of weeping ;
Life o'er death is triumph keeping,
  'Tis the time for joyance now !

Jesu Victor, life bestowing !
Jesu, Way to true life going !
Through Thy death death's self o'erthrowing !
At Thy Paschal feast o'erflowing
  Grant us in full trust a place !
Bread of life and Water living !
Vine, the true Vine, much fruit giving !
Feed us, cleanse us from sin's striving,
That, at second death arriving,
  We escape it through Thy grace ! Amen.

XV.

ASCENSIO.

POSTQUAM hostem et inferna
Spoliavit, ad superna
Christus redit gaudia;
Angelorum ascendenti
Sicut olim descendenti
Parantur obsequia.

Super astra sublimatur;
Non apparet, absentatur
Corporis præsentia;
Cuncta tamen moderatur,
Cujus Patri coæquatur
Honor et potentia.

Modo victor, modo tutus,
Est in cœlo constitutus
Rector super omnia.
Non est rursum moriturus,
Nec per mortem mandaturus
Hominum contagia.

XV.

ASCENSION.

SATAN and the realms infernal
Having spoiled, to joys supernal
Christ returneth back once more:
As His upward way He wendeth,
As before, when He descendeth,
Angels set them to adore.

As above the stars He goeth,
Here no more Himself He showeth,
Bodily, to mortal sight;
But all rule to Him is given,
Who is with His Sire in Heaven
One in majesty and might.

Victor now, from perils warded,
He in heaven hath been accorded
Empire over all therein:
Nevermore shall He be dying,
Nevermore through death supplying
Means to purify man's sin.

Semel enim incarnatus,
Semel passus, semel datus
  Pro peccatis hostia,
Nullam feret ultra pœnam,
Nam quietem habet plenam
  Cum summa lætitia.

Cum recessit, ita dixit,
Intimavit et infixit
  Talia discipulis:
"Ite, mundum circuite,
Universos erudite
  Verbis et miraculis.

"Nam ad Patrem meum ibo;
Sed sciatis quod redibo:
  Veniet Paraclitus
Qui desertos et loquaces,
Et securos, et audaces
  Faciet vos penitus.

"Super ægros et languentes
Manus vestras imponentes,
  Sanitatem dabitis;
Universas res nocentes,
Inimicos et serpentes
  Et morbos fugabitis.

Once for all He took our nature,
Once He suffered, once, a creature,
  Was for sin content to die :
Further pain shall He know never,
But, in perfect peace for ever,
  Compass endless joys on high.

Thus He spake, as He ascended;
These things straitly He commanded,
  And impressed upon His own :
"Go through all the world and preach ye,
Every nation therein teach ye
  Both by word and wonder done.

"For I go unto My Father,
To return, as ye may gather,
  Since shall come a Comforter,
Who shall make you bold and fearless,
Of all consequences careless,
  Eloquent in speech and clear.

"Those laid low by sickness on them,
When ye lay your hands upon them,
  Shall their former health regain:
All things hurtful and annoying,
With all deadly snakes, destroying,
  Ye shall drive out plagues and pain.

"Qui fidelis est futurus
Et cum fide suscepturus
  Baptismi remedium,
In peccatis erit purus
Et cum justis habiturus
  Sempiternum gaudium." Amen.

"Whosoever but believeth,
And with simple faith receiveth
  Baptism's sure remedy,
Shall be cleansed from all transgression,
And have with the saints possession
  Of eternal joys on high!" Amen.

XVI.

PENTECOSTE.

LUX jucunda, lux insignis,
Qua de throno missus ignis
In Christi discipulos
Corda replet, linguas ditat,
Ad concordes nos invitat
Linguæ cordis modulos.

Christus misit quod promisit
Pignus sponsæ, quam revisit
Die quinquagesima;
Post dulcorem melleum
Petra fudit oleum,
Petra jam firmissima.

In tabellis saxeis,
Non in linguis igneis
Lex de monte populo;
Paucis cordis novitas
Et linguarum unitas
Datur in cœnaculo.

XVI.

WHITSUNTIDE.

DAY delightful! day most noted!
When o'er Christ's disciples floated
Fire sent from the throne on high,
Filling hearts and tongues endowing,
And on hearts and tongues bestowing
Words and thoughts in harmony!

Christ, as once His word had spoken,
Sent His spouse a pledge and token,
Coming back the fiftieth day.
After streams of honey sweet
Oil that rock poured forth from it,
Which is now man's firmest stay.

From the mount to Jewry came
God's law, not in tongues of flame,
But on tables wrought from stone:
In a furnished upper room,
Given but to few, there come
Hearts renewed, and tongues as one.

O quam felix, quam festiva
Dies, in qua primitiva
Fundatur ecclesia!
Vivæ sunt primitiæ
Nascentis ecclesiæ,
Tria primum millia.

Panes legis primitivi
Sub una sunt adoptivi
Fide duo populi:
Se duobus interjecit
Sicque duos unum fecit
Lapis, caput anguli.

Utres novi, non vetusti,
Sunt capaces novi musti;
Vasa parat vidua;
Liquorem dat Eliseus;
Nobis sacrum rorem Deus,
Si corda sunt congrua.

Non hoc musto vel liquore,
Non hoc sumus digni rore,
Si discordes moribus.
In obscuris vel divisis
Non potest hæc Paraclisis
Habitare cordibus.

O the joy and jubilation
Of that day, when first foundation
  Of the early Church was laid:
  When the Church, then first begun,
  Souls three thousand to it won,
  Lively first-fruits of it made.

Thus one faith binds earth's two nations,
Like the early dispensation's
  Twofold offering of bread:
The Head Corner-stone two races
By His presence interlaces,
  And thus one the two are made.

In new bottles, not in olden,
Must the new-made wine be holden:
  Brings the widow but the cruse;
Oil is by Elijah given:
So doth God for dew from heaven
  Hearts, if fitting vessels, use.

Of this wine or oil before Thee,
Of this dew, are we unworthy,
  If we have not peace within:
Not in hearts 'gainst God rebelling,
Can this Comforter be dwelling,
  Nor in those made dark through sin.

Consolator alme, veni;
Linguas rege, corda leni;
Nihil fellis aut veneni
  Sub tua præsentia.
Nil jocundum, nil amœnum.
Nil salubre, nil serenum,
Nihil dulce, nihil plenum,
  Nisi tua gratia.

Tu lumen es et unguentum,
Tu cœleste condimentum
Aquæ ditans elementum
  Virtute mysterii.
Nova facti creatura,
Te laudamus mente pura,
Gratiæ nunc, sed natura
  Prius iræ filii.

Tu qui dator es et donum,
Tu qui condis omne bonum,
Cor ad laudem redde pronum,
Nostræ linguæ formans sonum
  In tua præconia.
Tu nos purga a peccatis,
Auctor ipse puritatis,
Et in Christo renovatis
Da perfectæ novitatis
  Plena nobis gaudia. Amen.

Come, Thou Comforter benignest!
Rule our hearts and tongues, Divinest!
Gall or poison, where Thou shinest,
May not any more be found:
There is not a joy or pleasure,
Health and rest are not a treasure,
Nought is sweet, all scant in measure,
Where Thy grace doth not abound.

Thou, for light and unction given,
A sweet savour sent from heaven,
Fillest simple water even
With a new mysterious power:
We, re-made by Thy creation,
Give Thee, with pure hearts, laudation;
Sons of grace, by generation
Sons of wrath who were before.

Thou, Who art both gift and giver,
Helping every good endeavour,
Cause our hearts to praise Thee ever,
And our lips, O let us never
But in blessing Thee employ:
Wash out every evil passion,
Who alone canst purge transgression!
And in Christ our souls refashion,
That we may, in full possession,
Our new nature's bliss enjoy! Amen.

XVII.

PENTECOSTE.

QUI procedis ab utroque,
Genitore Genitoque
Pariter, Paraclite,
Redde linguas eloquentes,
Fac ferventes
In te mentes
Flamma tua divite.

Amor Patris Filiique,
Par amborum et utrique
Compar et consimilis.
Cuncta reples, cuncta foves,
Astra regis, cœlum moves,
Permanens immobilis.

Lumen carum,
Lumen clarum,
Internarum
Tenebrarum

XVII.

WHITSUNTIDE.

COMFORTER, from both together,
From the Son and from the Father,
Who proceedest equally!
Eloquent our utterance render;
With Thy splendour
Bright engender
In our hearts true warmth for Thee.

Love of Father, Son, together;
Equal of them both; with either
One: the same in every part!
All Thou fillest, all Thou lovest,
Stars Thou rulest, heaven Thou movest,
Though immovable Thou art.

Light the dearest!
Light the clearest!
Off Thou scarest,
As Thou nearest,

Effugas caliginem;
Per te mundi sunt mundati;
Tu peccatum et peccati
Destruis rubiginem.

Veritatem notam facis
Et ostendis viam pacis
Et iter justitiæ.
Perversorum
Corda vitas,
Et bonorum
Corda ditas
Munere scientiæ.

Te docente
Nil obscurum,
Te præsente
Nil impurum;
Sub tua præsentia
Gloriatur mens jocunda;
Per te læta, per te munda
Gaudet conscientia.

Tu commutas elementa;
Per te suam sacramenta
Habent efficaciam:

From the heart its gloomy night:
All the pure Thou purifiest,
Thou it is that sin destroyest,
And its mildew's baleful blight.

Knowledge of the truth Thou spreadest;
On the way of peace Thou leadest,
And the path of righteousness.
From Thee thrusting
Hearts unruly,
Thou all trusting
Hearts and holy
Dost with gifts of wisdom bless.

When Thou teachest,
Nought obscure is!
Where Thou reachest,
Nought impure is;
And, if present Thou wilt be,
Hearts in Thee then blithely glory,
And the conscience joys before Thee,
Gladdened, purified, by Thee.

Elements their mystic dower,
Sacraments their saving power,
But through Thee alone possess:

Tu nocivam vim repellis,
Tu confutas et refellis
Hostium nequitiam.

Quando venis,
Corda lenis;
Quando subis
Atræ nubis
Effugit obscuritas;
Sacer ignis,
Pectus ignis;
Non comburis,
Sed a curis
Purgas, quando visitas.

Mentes prius imperitas
Et sopitas
Et oblitas
Erudis et excitas.
Foves linguas, formas sonum;
Cor ad bonum
Facit pronum
A te data charitas.

O juvamen
Oppressorum,
O solamen
Miserorum,

What can harm us Thou repellest,
Thou exposest and Thou quellest,
  Adversaries' wickedness.

    Where Thou lightest,
    Hearts are brightest;
    Gloom-enshrouded
    Clouds that brooded
  There, before Thee disappear;
    Fire all-holy!
    Hearts Thou truly
    Never burnest,
    But thence yearnest,
  When Thou comest, cares to clear.

Thou the heart, experience needing,
    Languor pleading,
    Little heeding,
  Dost instruct and rouse to right;
Speeches framing, tongues endowing,
    And bestowing
    Love all-glowing,
  Hearts Thou mak'st in good delight.

    Sustentation
      In dejection!
    Consolation
      In affliction!

Pauperum refugium,
Da contemptum terrenorum,
Ad amorem supernorum
Trahe desiderium!

Consolator
Et fundator,
Habitator
Et amator
Cordium humilium,
Pelle mala, terge sordes,
Et discordes
Fac concordes,
Et affer præsidium.

Tu qui quondam visitasti,
Docuisti, confortasti
Timentes discipulos,
Visitare nos digneris;
Nos, si placet, consoleris
Et credentes populos.

Par majestas
Personarum,
Par potestas
Est earum,

Only refuge of the poor!
Give us scorn for things terrestrial,
And to care for things celestial
Lead our longings more and more!

Comfort wholly,
Founder solely,
Inmate truly,
Lover throughly,
Of those hearts that bow to Thee!
Concord, where is discord, raising,
Ills thence chasing,
Guilt effacing,
Bring us true security!

Thou, Who once by visitation
Didst inform, and consolation
To Thy scared disciples give!
Deign Thou now to come unto us:
If it please Thee, comfort show us,
And all nations that believe!

One excelling
Greatness sharing,
One as well in
Power appearing,

Et communis Deitas:
Tu, procedens a duobus,
Coæqualis es ambobus;
In nullo disparitas.

Quia tantus es et talis
Quantus Pater est et qualis;
Servorum humilitas
Deo Patri, Filioque
Redemptori, Tibi quoque
Laudes reddat debitas. Amen.

But one God three Persons are.
Coming forth from two together,
Thou co-equal art with either,
No disparity is there.

Such as is the Father Thou art ;
Since so great and such Thou now art,
By Thy servants unto Thee,
With the Sire, and Son, in heaven
Our Redeemer, praise be given,
As is due, most reverently! Amen.

XVIII.

PENTECOSTE.

SIMPLEX in essentia,
Septiformis gratia,
Nos illustret Spiritus;
Cordis lustret tenebras
Et carnis illecebras
Lux emissa cœlitus!

Lex præcessit in figura,
Lex pœnalis, lex obscura,
Lumen evangelicum.
Spiritalis intellectus,
Litterali fronde tectus,
Prodeat in publicum!

Lex de monte populo,
Paucis in cœnaculo
Nova datur gratia.
Situs docet nos locorum,
Præceptorum vel donorum
Quæ sit eminentia.

XVIII.

WHITSUNTIDE.

MAY the Spirit on us shine,
One in essence all-divine,
Septiform in gifts of grace!
May His beams from Heaven's height
Flood the darkened heart with light
And our lusts' ensnaring ways!

First the penal Law came, clouded
O'er with types, in mystery shrouded,
Ere the Gospel light shone forth.
'Neath the foliage of the letter
May the spirit, free from fetter,
Of that Gospel spread o'er earth!

From the Mount the Law was given
Unto all; new grace from Heaven
In a chamber to a few;
The position of which places
Brings out the respective graces
Of their laws and gifts to view.

Ignis, clangor buccinæ,
Fragor cum caligine,
   Lampadum discursio,
Terrorem incutiunt
Nec amorem nutriunt,
   Quem effudit unctio.

      Sic in Sina
      Lex divina
   Reis est imposita;
      Lex timoris,
      Non amoris,
   Puniens illicita.

Ecce patres præelecti
Dii recentes sunt effecti:
   Culpæ solvunt vincula.
Pluunt verbo, tonant minis;
Novis linguis et doctrinis
   Consonant miracula.

Exhibentes ægris curam,
Morbum damnant, non naturam.
   Persequentes scelera,
Reos premunt et castigant:
Modo solvunt, modo ligant,
   Potestate libera.

Flames of fire, the trump's loud sound,
Din and darkness all around,
  Bickering lightnings sent abroad,
Strike wild terror to the heart,
Nor the fostering love impart,
  Which that unction hath outpoured.

      Thus were given
      Out of heaven
  Laws to sinners from the Mount;
      Laws of terror,
      Chastening error,
  Making love of small account.

By the fathers, pre-elected,
God-like works are now effected;
  They unloose sin's galling bond:
Rain their words, their threatenings thunder,
With their words their works of wonder,
  New and startling, correspond.

Caring for each sickly creature,
They condemn disease, not nature;
  Punishing iniquity,
Sinners they strike down and chasten;
Chains they loosen, chains they fasten,
  With a power from limit free.

Typum gerit Jubilei
Dies iste, si diei
  Requiris mysteria,
  In quo, tribus millibus
  Ad fidem currentibus,
  Pullulat Ecclesia.

Jubilæus est vocatus
Vel *dimittens* vel *mutatus*,
Ad priores vocans status
  Res distractas libere.
Nos distractos sub peccatis,
Liberet lex charitatis
Et perfectæ libertatis
  Dignos reddat munere. Amen.

Like a Jubilee appeareth
The appearance this day weareth,—
If its mystery thou would'st know;—
When three thousand souls make haste
'Mongst believers to be classed,
And the Church doth thrive and grow.

"Jubilee" is a provision
Made for *change* or for *remission*,
Freely to their first condition
Calling those in misery.
May the law, by love enacted,
Freeing us, by sin distracted,
Make us, to its gifts attracted,
Fit for perfect liberty! Amen.

XIX.

PENTECOSTE.

SPIRITUS
 Paraclitus,
Procedens divinitus,
 Manet ante sæcula;
 Populis,
 Discipulis
Ad salutem sedulis
 Pacis dedit oscula.

 Hodie
 Cum tertiæ
Surgit hora, veniæ
 Fit ampla donatio;
 Criminum
 Est hominum
Per actorem luminum
 Facta relaxatio.

 Micuit,
 Aperuit,
Viros fortes imbuit

XIX.

WHITSUNTIDE.

THE Spirit dear,
That Comforter,
Who, before all ages were,
By procession came from God,
On a race,
That sought His face,
Striving for His saving grace,
Hath the kiss of peace bestowed.

On this day,
When its first ray
The third hour doth display,
Comes full pardon's gift so bright,
Which is then
For all their sin
Freely offered to all men
By the Father of all light.

Its bright sheen
Was fully seen,
And inspired bold dauntless men

Suavis refectio;
Irruit
Et mituit
Et eosdem docuit
Suo magisterio.

Fragiles,
Indociles
Et adhuc inutiles,
Sermonum inopia,
Utiles,
Amabiles
Et amici probabiles
Facti sunt ex gratia.

Tenere,
Non temere,
Dilectis occurrere
Vult ita benignitas;
Propere
Consumere
Culpas vult et tergere
Non exstincta caritas.

Audio
Cum gaudio

With a sweet refreshment there;
Yea, did tame
With rushing flame,
And instruct and teach the same
In its learning rich and rare.

Men, before
Devoid of lore,
Weak and frail, and lacking power
Through the lack of eloquence,
Useful prove,
Friends worthy love,
And beloved where'er they move,
Through the grace it doth dispense.

Feelingly,
Not fearfully,
Thus would true benignity
To its well-belovéd come:
Instantly
Sin's infamy
Never-failing charity
Would wipe off us and consume.

O mine ear
With joy doth hear,

Quod ejus auxilio
  Sit tanta felicitas
Cum tanto tripudio . . .

Cesset avaritia,
  Fugetur iniquitas,
Cesset insolentia,
  Cesset infidelitas !

Sit in ipsa veritas ;
  Mentem cum modestia
Scrutetur humilitas,
  Gratiam pro gratia.

Reddat universitas
  Ut Christi familia
Quam commendat sanctitas
  Sit semper innoxia !

Sit in ipsa veritas,
  Sit peccati nescia,
Sit perennis claritas
  In cœlesti patria ! Amen.

That, whene'er His help is near,
  Such untold felicity
We shall meet with bounding feet . . .

Let all avarice vanish hence,
  Far away, wrong-doing ! flee :
No more pride and insolence,
  No more infidelity !

Let the truth still hold its place,
  And let but humility
Search the conscience,—grace for grace,—
  With all meekness modestly.

May the All in All so bless
  Christ the Lord's own family,
That it, marked by holiness,
  Be from ills for ever free !

Let the truth there hold its place,
  Let it sin ne'er understand :
Let its brightness never cease
  In the heavenly fatherland ! Amen.

XX.

PENTECOSTE.

VENI, summe consolator,
Spes salutis, vitæ dator,
Adsit tua gratia!
Dulcis ardor, ros divine,
Bonitatis gĕrmine
Eadem substantia.

Ab utroque derivatus
Et a neutro separatus,
Ad utrumque colligatus
Sempiterno fœdere;
Ros et vapor utriusque,
Donet Pater Filiusque
Quod effluas ad nos usque
Largifluo munere.

Rorem audis et vaporem,
Crede simul et odorem
Quo Deus discernitur.

XX.

WHITSUNTIDE.

COME, our comfort's chief reviver !
Hope of saving-health, Life-giver !
May Thy grace here present be !
Pleasant heat, dew from above !
Outgrowth from the God of love !
One with it substantially !

Who from both proceedest, neither
Canst be separate from either,
Linked with both of them together
By an everlasting tie ;
Dew and breath of both in heaven !
By both Sire and Son be given
Of Thy Spirit to us even
In rich plenty from on high.

Of this dew and breath thou hearest ;
Deem Him scent too, whereby clearest
Is His Godhead to us shown.

Rorem istum quem emittit
Qui plus gustat, magis sitit,
    Nec ardor reprimitur.

Plebs ut sacra renascatur,
Per hunc unda consecratur,
Cui super ferebatur
    In rerum exordium,
Fons, origo pietatis,
Fons emundans a peccatis,
Fons de fonte Deitatis,
    Fons sacrator fontium!

De salice sine lignis
Hædum vorat manans ignis
    Azymaque pariter;
Ignis dispar elementis,
In altari nostræ mentis
    Accendaris jugiter!

Umbrâ septem mulierum
Figuraris ipsum verum,
Idem ipse forma rerum,
    Septiformis Spiritus!
Speciebus designaris,
Nec specie variaris:
Absit unquam ut dicaris
    Speciei deditus!

As this dew, that from it bursteth,
Tastes man more, the more he thirsteth
    With a thirst that nought tones down.

For the world's regeneration
It to water consecration
Gave, on which at the creation,
    O'er its surface borne, it sate.
Fountain, source of love's devotion!
Fountain, cleansing sinful motion!
Fountain from the Godhead's ocean,
    That all founts doth consecrate!

Fire, unfed by fuel, flowing
From the rod with ardent glowing
    That devours both kid and bread!
Fire, unlike all fire, O may the
Altar of our soul, we pray Thee,
    Ever with Thy flame be fed!

Darkly by the women seven
Art Thou figured, Truth of Heaven!
Inner life to all things given!
    Spirit, Sevenfold in grace!
Thee all various types betoken,
Though Thy oneness be unbroken;
Nor of Thee may it be spoken,
    That a type can Thee embrace.

Ignis vive, vivax unda,
Munda sinus et fecunda,
Subministra gratiam;
Caritatis tactos igne,
Nosmet tibi fac benigne
Sanctitatis hostiam.

Patris, Nati pium flamen,
Vitiorum medicamen,
Fessis esto sublevamen,
Mœstis consolatio.
Castus amor et honestus,
Æstus ardens, sed modestus,
Quos urit ardor incestus
Tua sanet unctio.

Vox non sono designata,
Vox subtilis, vox privata,
Vox beatis inspirata,
O vox dulcis, O vox grata,
Sona nostris mentibus!
Lux depellens falsitatem,
Lux inducens veritatem,
Vitam atque sanitatem
Et æternam claritatem
Nobis confer omnibus. Amen.

Fire of life and life's bright river!
Cleanse and fertilize hearts ever,
    Giving grace in everything;
Touched with fire of true love, take us
To Thee, and in mercy make us
    Holiness's offering!

Sire and Son's blest emanation!
Be from sin our restoration,
When worn out, our sustentation,
    And our comfort, when we mourn!
Love both pure and noble truly!
Heat that warms, but ne'er unduly!
May Thine unction heal those throughly,
    Who with unchaste ardour burn!

Voice, that doth no sounds deliver!
Still small voice, that whisperest ever,
Saints inspiring to endeavour!
Voice of joy and sweetness! never
    Cease to sound within our heart!
Light, away all falsehood driving!
Light, to truth incentive giving!
Grant that—life, health, thence deriving,—
Of Thy brightness ever-living
    All of us may have our part! Amen.

XXI.

TRINITAS.

TRINITATEM simplicem,
Trinum Deum, non triplicem,
Supplex colat ecclesia!
Trinitatis
In creatis
Interlucent rebus vestigia.

Mens in Deum consurgat sobria!
Genitoris et Geniti
Spiritusque Paracliti
Gratia
Nobis sacra revelet mysteria.

Tres personæ sunt, et plura
Quæ personas distingunt mysteria.
Tres idem sunt in natura,
Quod una nec tribus minor singula.

Trium posse, scire, velle paria,
In personis tribus et distantia.
—Sit par reverentia
Tribus, et uni gloria! Amen.

XXI.

TRINITY.

TO the Trine God, not Gods three,
The Trinity in Unity,
Let the Church now bow the knee!
All creation
Indication,
Clear and lucid, gives of a Trinity.

Let the sober mind up to God then rise!
Of the Father and of the Son,
With the Paraclete Spirit one,
To our eyes
May God's grace reveal all the mysteries!

There are Persons three, and many
Mysteries marking these Persons distinctively:
One by nature, all and any,
Neither is separately less than all the three.

Equal in all Three is knowledge, power, and will,
Yet in their three Persons is there difference still:
—Equal reverence to the Three,
To the One all glory, be! Amen.

XXII.

TRINITAS.

PROFITENTES Unitatem
Veneremur Trinitatem
Pari reverentia,
Tres Personas asserentes
Personali differentes
A se differentia.

Hæc dicuntur *relative*,
Quum sint unum *substantive*,
Non tria principia.
Sive dicas tres vel tria,
Simplex tamen est *usia*,
Non triplex essentia.

Simplex esse, simplex posse,
Simplex velle, simplex nosse,
Cuncta simplicia.
Non unius quam duarum
Sive trium Personarum
Minor efficacia.

XXII.

TRINITY.

WE, the Unity confessing,
Must the Trinity be blessing
In our worship equally;
In three Persons thus believing;
Difference 'twixt them each perceiving
In their Personality.

Relatively of these speak we,
Substantively but one make we,
Nor three Persons in them see;
Call them three or threefold, never
But one substance are they ever,
Neither in their essence three.

One in being, One in power,
One in will and wisdom's dower,
One in all respects they be:
Of all these three Persons, either
One, or two, or all together,
Are Almighty equally.

Pater, Proles, Sacrum Flamen,
Deus unus : sed hi tamen
Habent quædam propria.
Una virtus, unum numen,
Unus splendor, unum lumen,
Hoc una quod alia.

Patri Proles est æqualis,
Nec hoc tollit personalis
Amborum distinctio.
Patri compar Filioque,
Spiritalis ab utroque
Procedit connexio.

Non humana ratione
Capi possunt hæ Personæ,
Nec harum discretio.
Non hic ordo temporalis,
Non hic situs, aut localis
Rerum circumscriptio.

Nil in Deo præter Deum,
Nulla causa præter eum
Qui causat causalia.
Effectiva vel formalis
Causa Deus, et finalis,
Sed nunquam materia

Father, Son, and Spirit Holy,
Are one God, but each hath truly
Some peculiar property:
One their goodness, one their might, is;
One their glory, one their light, is;
One are they entirely.

Equal are the Son and Father,
But from this we may not gather
That their Persons are the same:
One with Son and Father either,
Not from one, but both together,
The connecting Spirit came.

These three Persons that we mention
Are beyond man's comprehension,
As the difference each one shows:
Time and place alike unbounded
Are for them, and unsurrounded
By the limits nature knows.

Naught but God God's self compriseth,
Nor from other cause ariseth,
Cause of all causality:
Though the cause, all things respecting,
Formal, final, and effecting,
Immaterial is He.

Digne loqui de Personis
Vim transcendit rationis,
Excedit ingenia.
Quid sit gigni, quid processus,
Me nescire sum professus :
Sed fide non dubia.

Qui sic credit, ne festinet,
Et a via non declinet
Insolerter regia.
Servet fidem, formet mores,
Non declinet ad errores
Quos damnat Ecclesia.

Nos in fide gloriemur,
Nos in una modulemur
Fidei constantia :
Trinæ sit laus Unitati,
Sit et simplæ Trinitati
Coæterna gloria ! Amen.

To describe these Persons duly
Far transcends man's reason truly,
And exceeds his wit as well:
What that birth is, that procession,
Though faith doubts not, my confession
Must be that I cannot tell.

Who believes this, nought dismayeth;
He ne'er ignorantly strayeth
From this creed's right royal road;
Keeps the faith, his life makes purer,
Not declining into error
Censured by the Church of God.

In this faith then let us glory,
And in one consistent story
Hold it in its verity:
Praise be to the Triune Godhead;
To the Three in One included
Co-eternal glory be! Amen.

XXIII.

DEDICATIO ECCLESIÆ.

QUAM DILECTA TABERNACULA DOMINI VIRTUTUM, ET ATRIA!

QUAM electi
Architecti,
Tuta ædificia,
Quæ non movent,
Imo fovent
Ventus, flumen, pluvia!

Quam decora fundamenta
Per concinna sacramenta
Umbræ præcurrentia!
Latus Adæ dormientis
Evam fundit, in manentis
Copulæ primordia.

Arca ligno fabricata
Noe servat, gubernata
Mundi per diluvium.

XXIII.

ON THE DEDICATION OF A CHURCH.

O HOW LOVELY ARE THE COURTS DIVINE OF THE LORD OF HOSTS, HIS HALLOWED SHRINE!

O HOW skilled the
Hands that build thee;
How secure thy walls remain;
Ne'er subverted,
But supported
Rather by wind, flood, and rain!

O how comely thy foundations,
By deep mysteries' celebrations
Shadowing forth the coming day!
Adam, when in sleep reclining,
From his side pours Eve, beginning
Thus a bond to last for aye.

Noah, in ark of wood constructed,
O'er that flood is safe conducted,
Which did all the world destroy.

Prole sera tandem fœta,
Anus Sara ridet læta,
Nostrum lactans gaudium.

Servus bibit qui legatur
Et camelus adaquatur
Ex Rebeccæ hydria.
Hæc inaures et armillas
Aptat sibi, ut per illas
Virgo fiat congrua.

Synagoga supplantatur
A Jacob, dum devagatur
Nimis freta litteræ.
Liam lippam latent multa:
Quibus Rachel videns fulta,
Pari nubit fœdere.

In bivio tegens nuda,
Geminos parit ex Juda
Thamar diu vidua.
Hic Moyses a puella,
Dum se lavat, in fiscella
Reperitur scirpea.

Hic mas agnus immolatur,
Quo Israel satiatur,
Tinctus ejus sanguine.

Great with offspring long awaited,
Aged Sarah laughs, elated,
Giving milk to feed our joy.

Thirst the servant-legate slaketh,
And its fill his camel taketh,
From Rebecca's water-pail.
She, as rings and chains she weareth,
Fitly thus herself prepareth
To assume the bridal veil.

Since it so the letter vaunteth,
Jacob now the Law supplanteth,
Whilst it roams forth far and wide.
Rachel, since she sees much hidden
From Leah's tender sight, is bidden
To an equal rank as bride.

Tamar, long a widow biding,
By the way her features hiding,
Doth twin-sons to Judah bear.
Here in basket made of rushes
Moses see, who, while she washes,
Was perceived by maiden fair.

Here the male lamb, immolated,
Wherewith Israel's tribes are sated,
And besprinkled with its blood.

Hic transitur rubens unda,
Ægyptios sub profunda
Obruens voragine.

Hic est urna manna plena,
Hic mandata legis dena,
Sed in arca fœderis.
Hic sunt ædis ornamenta,
Hic Aaron indumenta
Quæ præcedit poderis.

Hic Urias viduatur,
Bethsabee sublimatur,
Sedis consors regiæ.
Hæc regi varietate
Vestis astat deauratæ,
Sicut regum filiæ.

Huc venit Austri regina,
Salomonis quam divina
Condit sapientia.
Hæc est nigra sed formosa,
Myrrhæ et thuris fumosa,
Virga pigmentaria.

Hæc futura
Quæ figura

Here the Red Sea, safe passed over,
Which the Egyptian host did cover
With its deep devouring flood.

Here the pot that manna filleth;
Here the Decalogue God willeth,
In the ark of covenant bound.
Here the Temple's decorations;
Aaron's robes for ministrations,
Chief the one that sweeps the ground.

Here his wife Uriah loseth;
Here the king for consort chooseth
Bathsheba, his throne to share.
As she by him takes her station,
Dons she gold's rich decoration,
Such as monarchs' daughters wear.

Hither Sheba's queen progresseth,
She, whom Solomon impresseth
With his wisdom all-divine:
Black she is, but comely; blending
Charms, as when in smoke ascending
Myrrh and frankincense combine.

Things forth-coming,
Darkly looming,

Obumbravit,
Reseravit
Nobis dies gratiæ :
Jam in lecto
Cum dilecto
Quiescamus
Et psallamus :
Adsunt enim nuptiæ.

Quarum tonat initium
In tubis epulantium
Et finis per psalterium.

Sponsum millena millia
Una canunt melodia,
Sine fine dicentia :
Alleluia !

'Neath types shaded,
Are paraded
Plainly by this day of grace:
With the dear one
Lying near one,
Rest we, raising
Psalms of praising;
For the marriage now takes place.

On first assembling for the feast
Is heard the trumpets' thrilling blast;
Sweet psalteries' notes ring forth at last.

The Bridegroom in ten thousand ways
These myriad minstrels hymn, whose lays
Are still the same, as still they raise
Their Alleluia's endless praise!

XXIV.

DEDICATIO ECCLESIÆ.

REX Salomon fecit templum,
Quorum instar et exemplum
Christus et Ecclesia.
Hujus hic est imperator,
Fundamentum et fundator,
Mediante gratia.

Quadri templi fundamenta
Marmora sunt, instrumenta
Parietum paria;
Candens flos est castitatis,
Lapis quadrus in prælatis
Virtus et constantia.

Longitudo,
Latitudo,
Templique sublimitas,
Intellecta
Fide recta,
Sunt fides, spes, caritas.

XXIV.

ON THE DEDICATION OF A CHURCH.

SOLOMON, the King, a Temple
Built, whose pattern and example
Christ, with Holy Church, appears:
He, its founder and foundation,
Sway, through grace's mediation,
As the Church's ruler bears.

Squarely built, this Temple's bases
Are of marble; each wall's space is
Formed of stones cut evenly:
Chastity's fair flower there twineth;
Each squared stone therein combineth,
Prelates' nerve and constancy.

Its far-reaching
Length, and stretching
Width, and height that tempts the sky,
Faith explaining
The true meaning,
Are Faith, Hope, and Charity.

Sed tres partes sunt in Templo
Trinitatis sub exemplo
Ima, summa, media :
Ima signat vivos cunctos,
Et secunda jam defunctos,
Redivivos tertia.

Sexagenos quæque per se,
Sed et partes universæ
Habent lati cubitos :
Harum trium tres conventus
Trinitati dant concentus
Unitati debitos.

Templi cultus
Extat multus,
Cinnamomus
Odor domus,
Myrrha, stacte, casia ;
Quæ bonorum
Decus morum
Atque bonos
Precum sonos
Sunt significantia.

In hac casa
Cuncta vasa

Tripartite is this fair Temple,
After the Triune's example,
With first, third, and middle floor:
First, the living signifying;
Second, those in death now lying,
Third, those raised to life once more.

All the parts together rated,
Or alone, are calculated
Threescore cubits wide to be:
Triply do these three, thus blending,
Harmonize with the transcending
Trinity in Unity.

Gorgeous ritual
And perpetual
Scents, sweet smelling,
Fill God's dwelling,
Cassia, myrrh, and cinnamon;
Signifying
Never-dying
Christian graces,
Prayers, and praises,
Grateful offerings at His throne.

In this palace
Is each chalice

Sunt ex auro,
De thesauro
Præelecto penitus:
Nam magistros
Et ministros
Decet doctos
Et excoctos
Igne Sancti Spiritus.

Sic ex bonis
Salomonis
Quæ Rex David
Præparavit
Fiunt ædificia;
Nam in lignis
Res insignis
Vivit Tyri,
Cujus viri
Tractant artificia.

Nam ex gente Judæisque
Sicut Templum ab utrisque
Conditur Ecclesia:
Christe, qui hanc et hos unis,
Lapis huic et his communis,
Tibi laus et gloria! Amen.

A gold measure
From the treasure
Pre-elected secretly:
For all teachers'
Minds, and preachers',
Throughly furnished,
Purged, and burnished,
By the Spirit's fire should be.

Thus with treasure,
David's pleasure
Had collected,
Is erected
Solomon's great sanctuary;
But the dwelling,
All excelling,—
Timber sending,
Craftsmen lending,—
Tyre's art fashioned cunningly.

Formed of Jew and Gentile races,
Builds the Church her holy places,
As did both the Temple raise.
Christ, Who both in one unitest!
Corner-stone of each! the brightest
Glory be to Thee and praise. Amen.

XXV.

DEDICATIO ECCLESIÆ.

CLARA chorus dulce pangat voce nunc alleluia,
Ad æterni Regis laudem qui gubernat omnia !

Cui nos universalis sociat Ecclesia,
Scala nitens et pertingens ad poli fastigia ;

Ad honorem cujus læta psallamus melodia,
Persolventes hodiernas laudes illi debitas.

O felix aula, quam vicissim
Confrequentant agmina cœlica,
Divinis verbis alternatim
Jungentia mellea cantica !

XXV.

ON THE DEDICATION OF A CHURCH.

LET our choir now loudly join their Alleluia's brightest strains,
The eternal Monarch praising, who o'er all creation reigns!

Unto Him the universal Church uniteth us in love,
Like a shining ladder reaching to the heights of heaven above.

To His honour psalms of gladness we in tuneful strains upraise,
Paying thus the proper tribute to Him of our daily praise.

O hall of bliss! where, in due order,
Troops of angels gather continually;
And with divine words, alternating,
Join sweet strains of ravishing melody!

Domus hæc, de qua vetusta sonuit historia
Et moderna protestatur Christum fari pagina :
" Quoniam elegi eam thronum sine macula,
Requies hæc erit mea per eterna sæcula."

Turris supra montem sita,
Indissolubili bitumine fundata
Vallo perenni munita,
Atque aurea columna
Miris ac variis lapidibus distincta,
Stylo subtili polita !

Ave, mater præelecta,
Ad quam Christus fatur ita
Prophetæ facundia :
" Sponsa mea speciosa,
Inter filias formosa,
Supra solem splendida !

" Caput tuum ut Carmelus,
Et ipsius comæ tinctæ regis uti purpura ;

'Tis the home of which the former Testament did
 sound the praise,
And of which the New declareth that 'tis Christ
 Himself that says:
"Seeing I have chosen this to be my throne of
 purity,
Henceforth through undying ages here my resting-
 place shall be!"

Tower! on a Mount erected,
And with cement that melteth not upon it founded,
By perennial walls protected,
And with pillared gold surrounded,
Of divers jewels, polished with fine skill, com-
 pounded,
For their rarity selected!

Elect Mother! hail! whom, blessing,
Christ is in these words addressing
 Of impassioned prophecy:
"Rise, my lovely spouse! the fairest
'Mongst earth's daughters thou appearest,
 Brighter than the sun on high!

"Lo! thy head is like Mount Carmel,
And the flowing locks upon it, as with regal purple,
 red:

Oculi ut columbarum,
Genæ tuæ punicorum ceu malorum fragmina !

" Collum tuum ut columna, turris et eburnea ;
Mel et lac sub lingua tua, favus stillans labia !"

Ergo nobis Sponsæ tuæ
Famulantibus, O Christe, pietate solita,
Clemens adesse digneris,
Et in tuo salutari nos ubique visita.

Ipsaque mediatrice, summe Rex, perpetue,
Voce pura
Flagitamus, da gaudere Paradisi gloria.
Alleluia !

Doves' eyes do thine eyes resemble;
Like a piece of a pomegranate are the temples of thine head.

"Like a column is thy neck and like an ivory tower's walls;
Milk and honey 'neath thy tongue, thy lips a comb whence honey falls."

Therefore still with us, the servants
Of Thy spouse, O Christ! we pray Thee, in Thy never-failing love
Kindly deign Thou to be present:
Everywhere with Thy salvation visit us from heaven above!

Through her mediation also, King Most High! perpetually
We implore Thee
Loudly, that with alleluias we 'midst joys of Paradise
May adore Thee!

XXVI.

DEDICATIO ECCLESIÆ.

JERUSALEM et Sion filiæ,
Cœtus omnis fidelis curiæ,
Melos pangas jugis lætitiæ,
Alleluia!
Christus enim desponsat hodie
Matrem nostram, norma justitiæ,
Quam de lacu traxit miseriæ,
Ecclesiam.

In Spiritus Sancti clementia,
Sponsa sponsi lætatur gratia:
A reginis, laudum cum gloria,
Felix dicta.
Dos ut datur, crescit lætitia:
Quæ dos! quanta! triplex potentia,
Tangens cœlum, terram et stygia
Judicia.

Mira loquar, sed sanum credere:
Fœderatam tam largo munere,
De proprio produxit latere
Deus-Homo.

XXVI.

ON THE DEDICATION OF A CHURCH.

JERUSALEM and Sion's daughters fair !
And all the faithful crowd that worship there !
That ceaseless strain of tuneful joy prepare,
"Alleluia !"
For Christ, Who doth all righteousness display,
Is to our Mother-Church espoused to-day,
That Church, whom He in love hath drawn away
From depths of woe.

Through the blest Spirit's mercy from above
The Bride rejoices in the Bridegroom's love :
Earth's queens with glorious praises doth she move
To call her blest.
'Mid greater joy still is her dowry given :
What ! and how great ! that threefold power, which heaven,
And earth below, and the dread judgments even
Of hell affects.

Belief is wise, though strange my tale :—that bride,
By gifts of such vast magnitude allied
To Him, was taken out of His own side
By the God-Man :

Formaretur ut sic Ecclesia
Figuravit in pari gloria
Adæ costis formata femina,
Hostis Eva.

Eva fuit noverca posteris:
Hæc est mater electi generis,
Vitæ portus, asylum miseris
Et tutela.
Pulchra, potens, partu mirabilis,
Ut luna, sol, fulget spectabilis,
Plus acie multo terribilis
Ordinata.

Multiplex est, singularis, una,
Generalis et individua;
Omnis ævi, sexus, simul una
Parit turmas.
Hæc signata Jordanis fluctibus;
Hæc quæ venit a terræ finibus,
Scientiam audire cominus
Salomonis.

Hæc typicis descripta sensibus,
Nuptiarum induta vestibus,
Cœli præest hodie civibus
Christo juncta.

That thus the Church should form and shape receive
In equal glory, we a type believe
Was *woman*, formed—source of our sorrow, Eve !—
From Adam's rib.

Eve a stepmother hath been to her seed ;
The Church to her elect a mother indeed,
Life's haven, an asylum in their need,
And sure defence.
She, beautiful and great, in birth divine,
Fair as the moon, clear as the sun doth shine ;
More terrible than armies' serried line,
With banners dight.

Multifold is she, yet but one alone ;
As all together, and each singly, known ;
Of every age and sex, yet only one ;
Troops she brings forth.
Jordan ! thy waves a type of her appear,
And she, that from the ends of earth drew near,
That, face to face, she might the wisdom hear
Of Solomon.

She, whom these types, when understood, portray,
Robed for her marriage-feast in bright array,
Presides o'er all the heavenly host to-day,
The bride of Christ.

O solemnis festum lætitiæ;
Quo unitur Christus Ecclesiæ,
In quo nostræ salutis nuptiæ
Celebrantur!

Cœtus felix, dulce convivium,
Lapsis ubi datur solatium,
Desperatis offertur spatium
Respirandi!
Justis inde solvuntur præmia,
Angelorum novantur gaudia,
Læta nimis quod facit gratia
Charitatis.

Ab æterno fons sapientiæ,
Intuitu solius gratiæ,
Sic prævidit in rerum serie
Hæc futura.
Christus ergo nos suis nuptiis,
Recreatos veris deliciis,
Interesse faciat gaudiis
Electorum! Amen.

O holy joy's bright feast-day in the skies,
Which joins the Church with Christ in marriage-ties!
That marriage-day, whose rite mankind allies
With saving-health!

O happy gathering! O sweet feast of heaven!
When consolation to the lapsed is given,
And to the sinner, to despair now driven,
A breathing-space!
Here their rewards are to the righteous paid,
And angels' joys, renewed again, displayed;
Feast, by the grace of charity thus made
Too full of joy!

The fount of wisdom from the first hath known,
Through the clear insight given by grace alone,
As the due course of things hath onward gone,
What is to be:
Therefore may Christ, by these His marriage-rites,
Make us, refreshed thereby with true delights,
Partake those joys to which His love invites
All His elect! Amen.

FOR SAINTS' DAYS.

XXVII.

S. ANDREAS.

XXX° NOVEMBRIS.

EXULTEMUS et lætemur
Et Andreæ delectemur
Laudibus apostoli;
Hujus fidem, dogma, mores,
Et pro Christo tot labores,
Digne decet recoli.

Hic ad fidem Petrum duxit,
Cui primum lux illuxit,
Joannis indicio.
Secus mare Galilææ,
Petri simul et Andreæ
Sequitur electio.

Ambo prius piscatores
Verbi fiunt assertores
Et formæ justitiæ.
Rete laxant in capturam
Vigilemque gerunt curam
Nascentis Ecclesiæ.

XXVII.

ST. ANDREW.

NOVEMBER 30TH.

LET us, shouts of gladness raising,
Now delighted to be praising
The Apostle Andrew be:
Whose faith, life, and doctrine precious,
With his mighty works for Jesus,
Should be honoured worthily.

He, who first the true light's glowing
Saw, at John the Baptist's showing,
Peter led the faith to see!
Then are Peter and his brother
Called along with one another
At the Sea of Galilee.

Fishermen till then, both preachers
Of the word become and teachers
Of the rules of righteousness:
Now a net to catch men loose they,
And a wary forethought use they
The young Church to guard and bless.

A fratre dividitur
Et in partes mittitur
Andreas Achäiæ.
In Andreæ retia
Currit, Dei gratia,
Magna pars provinciæ.

Fide, vita, verbo, signis,
Doctor pius et insignis,
Cor informat populi.
Ut Ægeas comperit
Quid Andreas egerit,
Iræ surgunt stimuli.

Mens secura, mens virilis,
Cüi præsens vita vilis,
Viget patientia.
Blandimentis aut tormentis,
Non enervat robur mentis
Judicis insania.

Crucem videns præparari,
Suo gestit conformari
Magistro discipulus.
Mors pro morte solvitur
Et crucis appetitur
Triumphalis titulus.

Andrew soon his brother leaves,
When commission he receives,
And is in Achaia placed :
Of which province a great part,
By God's grace convinced in heart,
To the nets of Andrew haste.

By his faith, life, signs, and speeches
This great, good, man's doctrine reaches
And reforms the people's heart.
When Ægeas findeth out
All that Andrew thus had wrought,
Forth his bitter wrath-stings start.

His staid heart and manly spirit,
Who in this life saw no mĕrit,
Stronger from endurance grow.
Flattering or tormenting either,
His insensate judge by neither
Can his strength of mind o'erthrow.

When he sees the cross preparing,
Like his Master, suffering sharing,
The disciple longs to be ;
For Christ's death he pays his own,
And for its triumphal crown
On the cross seeks eagerly.

In cruce vixit biduum,
Victurus in perpetuum :
Nec vult, volente populo,
Deponi de patibulo.

Hora fere dimidia
Luce perfusus nimia,
Cum luce, cum lætitia,
Pergit ad lucis atria.

O Andrea gloriose,
Cujus preces pretiosæ,
Cujus mortis luminosæ
    Dulcis est memoria ;
Ab hac valle lacrymarum
Nos ad illud lumen clarum,
Pie pastor animarum,
    Tua transfer gratia. Amen.

Upon the cross he lived two days,
Thenceforth to live in heaven always;
Nor, when the people wished, would he
Be lifted from the fatal tree.

Nigh half an hour upon that height
Bathed in a light exceeding bright,
In light, exulting at the sight,
He passes to the halls of light.

Andrew, crowned with endless glory!
Rich in prayer propitiatory!
Of whose brilliant death the story
'Tis so sweet in thought to trace!
From this vale of woe exceeding
To that light such radiance shedding,
Loving shepherd, spirits feeding!
O transport us by thy grace! Amen.

XXVIII.

S. NICOLAUS.

VI° DECEMBRIS.

CONGAUDENTES exultemus vocali concordia
Ad beati Nicolai festiva solemnia;

Qui in cunis adhuc jacens servando jejunia
A papillis cœpit summa promereri gaudia.

Adolescens amplexatur literarum studia,
Alienus et immunis ab omni lascivia.

Felix confessor,
Cujus fuit dignitatis vox de cœlo nuntia!
Per quam provectus,
Præsulatûs sublimatur ad summa fastigia.

XXVIII.

ST. NICHOLAS.

DECEMBER 6TH.

LET us all exult together, as with one united voice
We upon his solemn feast-day in St. Nicholas rejoice;

Who, whilst in his cradle lying, by observing duly fast,
Heavenly joys began to merit even at his mother's breast.

In his youth he chooses letters, that his study they may be,
To all evil lust a stranger, from all sinful passions free.

This blest confessor,
Whom, as worthy of the office, 'twas a voice from heaven praised,
Thereby exalted,
Amongst bishops to the very highest rank is forthwith raised.

Erat in ejus animo pietas eximia,
Et oppressis impendebat multa beneficia.

Auro per eum virginum tollitur infamia,
Atque patris earundem levatur inopia.

Quidam nautæ navigantes,
Et contra fluctuum sævitiam luctantes,
Navi pene dissoluta,
Jam de vita desperantes,
In tanto positi periculo, clamantes
Voces dicunt omnes una :

"O beate Nicolae,
Nos ad maris portum trahe
De mortis angustia.
Trahe nos ad portum maris,
Tu qui tot auxiliaris
Pietatis gratia."

Dum clamarent, nec incassum,
"Ecce!" quidam dicit, "assum

There was too in his character benevolence exceeding,
And many a bounty he bestowed, the tale of sorrow heeding.

With gold he saved some maidens, who had else vile lives been leading,
Relieving all their father's want, when help most sorely needing.

Certain sailors once, when sailing,
And fighting 'gainst fierce waves with struggles unavailing,
Shipwrecked nigh through stress of weather ;
Hope of life already failing,
Amid such dangers set, aloud their fate bewailing,
Lift their voices altogether :

"Blessed Nicholas ! O steer us
From the straits of death so near us
To the haven of the sea !
To that harbour in the distance
Draw us, who dost grant assistance
Through the grace of charity !"

"Lo !"—while thus they cried, nor vainly,—
"I am here !" a voice said plainly,

Ad vestra præsidia."
Statim aura datur grata
Et tempestas fit sedata :
Quieverunt maria.

Nos, qui sumus in hoc mundo,
Vitiorum in profundo
Jam passi naufragia,
Gloriose Nicolae,
Ad salutis portum trahe,
Ubi pax et gloria.

Ex ipsius tumba manat
Unctionis copia,
Quæ infirmos omnes sanat
Per ejus suffragia.

Ipsam nobis unctionem
Impetres ad Dominum,
Prece pia,
Quæ sanavit læsionem
Multorum peccaminum
In Maria.

Hujus festum celebrantes gaudeant per sæcula,
Et coronet eos Christus post vitæ curricula !
Amen dicant omnia !

"To watch o'er you and to aid!"
Instantly blow favouring breezes,
Instantly the tempest ceases,
And to rest the sea is laid.

We, now in this world abiding,
Have been wrecked, as we were riding
O'er the deep abyss of vice:
Draw us, Nicholas most glorious!
To the home of peace victorious,
To the port of Paradise!

From his tomb, to heal diseases,
Oil abundant floweth forth,
Which the sick from pain releases
Through his prayers' availing worth.

May we of the self-same ointment
Through thy pious prayer to God
Gain possession,
Which did by the Lord's appointment
Heal the wounds of Mary's load
Of transgression!

Let them joy throughout all ages, who observe this holy day,
And, when this life's course is ended, crowned in heaven by Christ be they!
Amen! let all creatures say!

XXIX.

S. STEPHANUS.

XXVI° DECEMBRIS.

HERI mundus exultavit
Et exultans celebravit
Christi natalitia ;
Heri chorus angelorum
Prosecutus est cœlorum
Regem cum lætitia.

Protomartyr et Levita,
Clarus fide, clarus vita,
Clarus et miraculis,
Sub hac luce triumphavit,
Et triumphans insultavit
Stephanus incredulis.

Fremunt ergo tanquam feræ,
Quia victi defecere
Lucis adversarii :
Falsos testes statuunt,
Et linguas exacuunt
Viperarum filii.

XXIX.

ST. STEPHEN.

DECEMBER 26TH.

YESTERDAY the world, elated,
Joyed, and, joying, celebrated
Christ the Saviour's natal day:
Yesterday, heaven's King surrounding,
Angel-choirs, his welcome sounding,
Sang to him with joyful lay.

Protomartyr and a deacon,
Faith's clear light and life's bright beacon,
For his wonder-works well known,
Stephen on this day all-glorious
Won the victory, and, victorious,
Trod the unbelievers down.

Thus, since those 'gainst light engaging,
Conquered, fail, behold them raging
Like wild beasts in their despair:
Lying witnesses they bring,
And with bitter words they sting,
Seed of vipers that they are!

Agonista, nulli cede,
Certâ certus de mercede,
Persevera, Stephane:
Insta falsis testibus,
Confuta sermonibus
Synagogam Satanæ.

Testis tuus est in cœlis,
Testis verax et fidelis,
Testis innocentiæ.
Nomen habes Coronati:
Te tormenta decet pati
Pro corona gloriæ.

Pro corona non marcenti
Prefer brevis vim tormenti!
Te manet victoria.
Tibi fiet mors natalis,
Tibi pœna terminalis
Dat vitæ primordia.

Plenus Sancto Spiritu,
Penetrat intuitu
Stephanus cœlestia.
Videns Dei gloriam,
Crescit ad victoriam,
Suspirat ad præmia.

Champion! yield to none, but ever
Persevere in thine endeavour,
Stephen! sure of sure reward:
Their false witnesses withstand,
And confute all Satan's band
By thine eloquence outpoured.

In the heavens thy Witness dwelleth;
Truly, faithfully, He telleth
How thou hast no evil done:
Since "a crown" for name thou bearest,
Suffering first thou fitly sharest,
Till thy glory-crown be won.

For that crown's unfading dower
Choose to bear brief torture's power;
There awaits thee victory!
Death new birth for thee portendeth,
And its pain, which quickly endeth,
Is the dawn of life to thee.

Full of the blest Spirit's grace,
Stephen into heaven's space
Penetrates with lightened eyes;
Gazing on God's glory, he
Waxes strong for victory,
Longing for its deathless prize.

En a dextris Dei stantem,
Jesum pro te dimicantem,
Stephane, considera:
Tibi cœlos reserari,
Tibi Christum revelari,
Clama voce liberâ.

Se commendat Salvatori,
Pro quo dulce ducit mori
Sub ipsis lapidibus.
Saulus servat omnium
Vestes lapidantium,
Lapidans in omnibus.

Ne peccatum statuatur
His, a quibus lapidatur,
Genu ponit, et precatur,
Condolens insaniæ:
In Christo sic obdormivit,
Qui Christo sic obedivit,
Et cum Christo semper vivit,
Martyrum primitiæ.

Quod sex suscitaverit
Mortuos in Africa,
Augustinus asserit,
Fama refert publica.

Lo! at God's own right hand standing,
Jesus, in thy cause contending,
    Stephen! lift thine eyes and see!
Cry that heaven now open lieth;
And that Christ thine eye descrieth
    Cry aloud in accents free!

To his Lord his soul commending,
Sweet he deems it at life's ending
    'Neath these stones for him to fall.
  Saul stands by and keeps the clothes
  Of each stoner as he throws,
    Stoning Stephen through them all.

That the Lord would not be laying
To his murderers' charge this slaying,
Stephen kneeleth down, and, praying,
  Mourns their mad and reckless deed:
So asleep in Christ fell Stephen,
Who had Christ to serve so striven,
And now lives with Christ in heaven,
  First-fruits of the martyrs' seed!

  That in Africa from death
    He six men to life revived,
  Is a fact Augustine saith,
    And one commonly believed.

Hujus, Dei gratia,
Revelato corpore,
Mundo datur pluvia
Siccitatis tempore.

Solo fugat hic odore
Morbos et dæmonia,
Laude dignus et honore
Jugique memoria.

Martyr, cujus est jocundum
Nomen in Ecclesia,
Languescentem fove mundum
Cœlesti fragrantia. Amen.

When, by God's grace, his remains
  From their grave to light were brought,
Then were given heavy rains
  On the earth in time of drought.

He by perfume rare alone
  Makes disease and demons flee,
And due praise and fame hath won
  With a deathless memory.

Martyr! whose sweet name doth live
  In the Church so pleasantly,
An enfeebled world revive
  With thy heavenly fragrancy! Amen.

XXX.

S. STEPHANUS.

XXVI° DECEMBRIS.

ROSA novum dans odorem,
Adornatum ampliorem
Regiæ cœlestis,
Ab Ægypto revocatur;
Illum sequi gratulatur
Cujus erat testis.

Genus nequam et infaustum
Qui se fecit holocaustum
Afficit indigne,
Et quod in Christum credit,
A quo tamen non recedit
Passionis igne.

Gaudet carne purpurata,
Flexo genu, voce grata,
Pro Judæis orans,
Ut non illis imputetur
Quia gratis pateretur,
Facinus ignorans.

XXX.

ST. STEPHEN.

December 26th.

LO! a rose, new odour shedding,
Bright with beauty, all exceeding,
From the halls of heaven,
Out of Egypt is invited,
And to follow Christ delighted,
After witness given.

An unhappy, evil nation
Treats its victim's self-oblation
In unworthy fashion,
And Christ's truths, for which he pleadeth;
Though therefrom he ne'er recedeth
Through his fiery passion.

In his bruised flesh he rejoices;
Bent his knee and soft his voice is,
For the Jews' race pleading,
That 'gainst them his causeless passion
Be not charged, of their transgression
Being thus unheeding.

Constitutum in spe certa
Certiorat res aperta,
Quando Jesum vidit
Stantem Patris in virtute;
Tunc ad petram pugnans tute
Pavidos allidit.

Uva, data torculari,
Vult pressuras inculcari
Ne sit infecunda;
Martyr optat petra teri,
Sciens munus adaugeri
Sanguinis in unda.

Nos qui mundi per desertum
Agitamur in incertum,
Stephanum sequamur,
Ut securi tanto duce
Trinitatis vera luce
Jugiter fruamur. Amen.

His hope's certain expectation
Is confirmed to demonstration,
  When he Christ perceiveth
In His Father's glory standing;
On the rock then, safe contending,
  Awe-struck foes he driveth.

As a grape, the wine-press feeding,
Would have wine pressed thence by treading,
  Lest it useless seemeth;
So the martyr stoning pleaseth,
Knowing his reward increaseth,
  As his life-blood streameth.

Let us, through earth's desert driven
Here and there, to follow Stephen
  In his course endeavour;
That, safe such a leader under,
We the Triune's true light yonder
  May enjoy for ever! Amen.

XXXI.

S. JOANNES EVANGELISTA.

XXVII° DECEMBRIS.

GRATULEMUR ad festivum,
Jocundemur ad votivum
Johannis præconium !
Sic versetur laus in ore,
Ne fraudetur cor sapore
Quo degustet gaudium.

Hic est Christi prædilectus,
Qui reclinans supra pectus
Hausit sapientiam ;
Huic in cruce commendavit
Matrem Christus ; hic servavit
Virgo viri nesciam.

Intus ardens caritate,
Foris lucens honestate,
Signis et eloquio,
Ut ab æstu criminali,
Sic immunis a pœnali,
Prodiit ex dolio.

XXXI.

ST. JOHN THE EVANGELIST.

DECEMBER 27TH.

ON his feast with gratulation
Joy we at John's exaltation,
As we pay our public vows!
Let the mouth so sing his praises,
That the relish which it raises
The glad heart may never lose.

This is he most loved by Jesus,
Who drank draughts of wisdom precious,
As he on His breast did lean:
To whom Mary was commended
From Christ's cross; who, virgin, tended
Her who had not known a man.

Inwardly with warm love glowing,
Outwardly bright virtue showing,
Eloquence and wonders wrought;
As by lust's consuming fever,
So by tortures' heat, touched never,
From the oil-vat came he out.

Vim veneni superavit,
Morti, morbis imperavit,
  Necnon et dæmonibus :
Sed vir tantæ potestatis,
Non minoris pietatis
  Erat tribulantibus.

Cum gemmarum partes fractas
Solidasset, has distractas
  Tribuit pauperibus.
Inexhaustum fert thesaurum,
Qui de virgis fecit aurum,
  Gemmas de lapidibus.

Invitatur ab amico
Convivari ; Christum dico
  Visum cum discipulis.
De sepulcro quo descendit,
Redivivus sic ascendit
  Frui summis epulis.

Testem habes populum,
Immo, si vis, oculum,
Quod ad ejus tumulum
Manna scatet, epulum
  De Christi convivio.

Poison's strength he overpowered,
Death, disease, beneath him cowered,
And the very devils too:
But the man, such power possessing,
Could no less bring health and blessing
Unto those in want and woe.

Broken gems by him were mended,
And their value was expended
On the poor, his pious loan.
He produces boundless treasure,
Who from tree-twigs at his pleasure
Fashioned gold, and gems from stone.

By a friend to banquet bidden,—
Christ, I mean, no longer hidden,
Seen with His disciples there,—
From the grave, where he was lying,
He arose in form undying,
In the heavenly feast to share.

There are crowds to testify,
Nay, yourself may trust your eye,
How that, where he once did lie,
Flows forth manna, a supply
From the table of the Lord.

Scribens evangelium,
Aquilæ fert proprium,
Cernens solis radium,
Scilicet principium,
Verbum in principio.

Hujus signis est conversa
Gens gentilis, gens perversa,
Gens totius Asiæ.
Hujus scriptis illustratur,
Illustrata solidatur
Unitas ecclesiæ.

Salve, salvi vas pudoris,
Vas cœlestis plenum roris,
Mundum intus, clarum foris,
Nobile per omnia.
Fac nos sequi sanctitatem;
Fac, per mentis puritatem,
Contemplari Trinitatem
In una substantia. Amen.

As he doth his Gospel write,
Eagle-like in upward flight,
He beholds the Light of Light,
Its primæval source, to wit,
"In the beginning was the Word!"

A perverse and heathen nation,
All of Asia's population,
To the faith his wonders won.
Illustrated by his writing,
Unity, the Church uniting,
Firmer ground now stands upon.

Vessel, hail! that no sin staineth!
Vessel, that heaven's dew containeth!
Which within quite pure remaineth,
Bright without, all dignity!
Cause us, like thee, to be holy,
And, with spirits chastened throughly,
Let us see the Godhead fully,
In one substance Persons three. Amen.

o

XXXII.

S. JOANNES EVANGELISTA.

XXVII° DECEMBRIS.

VERBI vere substantivi,
Caro cum sit in declivi
Temporis angustiâ,
In æternis verbum annis
Permanere, nos Johannis
Docet theologia.

Dum Magistri super pectus
Fontem haurit intellectûs
Et doctrinæ flumina,
Fiunt, ipso situ loci,
Verbo fides, auris voci,
Mens Deo contermina.

Unde mentis per excessus,
Carnis, sensûs super gressus
Errorumque nubila,
Contra veri solis lumen
Visum cordis et acumen
Figit velut aquila.

XXXII.

ST. JOHN THE EVANGELIST.

DECEMBER 27TH.

JOHN'S theology declareth,
Though on earth all flesh appeareth
To decline in swift decay,
That the Word's word self-existent,
Through all ages still consistent,
Will remain nor pass away.

As the loved disciple sinketh
On his Master's breast, and drinketh
Wisdom's fount and learning's stream,
From a posture so endearing
Word and faith, and speech and hearing,
Mind and God, converging seem.

By the flights of thought thence taken,—
Flesh and carnal sense forsaken,—
Far o'er error's cloudy night,
Eagle-like, by observation,
The true Sun's illumination,
Keeps his keen-eyed heart in sight.

Hebet sensus exsors styli,
Stylo scribit tam subtili,
    Fide tam catholica,
Ne de Verbo salutari
Posset quicquam refragari,
    Pravitas hæretica.

Verbum quod non potest dici,
Quod virtute creatrici
Cuncta fecit valde bona,
Iste dicit ab æterni
Patris nexu non secerni,
Nisi tantum in persona.

Quem Matthæus de intactæ
Matris alit casto lacte
Cum labore et ærumna;
Quem exaltat super cruce,
Cornu bovis, penna Lucæ,
Ut serpentem in columna;

Quem de mortis mausoleo
Vitæ reddit Marci leo,
Scissis petris, terra mota,
Hunc de Deo deum verum
ALPHA et Ω, Patrem rerum,
Solers scribit idiota.

Want of style the sense confuses,
But such subtlety John uses,
And so Catholic his faith,
That all heretics, depraving
Doctrines of that Word soul-saving,
Fail to gainsay aught he saith.

Lo! that Word, beyond expression,
Who all very good did fashion
By His power of creation,
From the eternal Sire appeareth
Undivided, John declareth,
Save in Personal relation.

Whom with chaste milk Matthew feedeth,
Which from virgin breasts proceedeth,
With much toil and trouble blended;
Whom that ox-horn, Luke's pen, placeth
On the cross and high upraiseth,
As the serpent was suspended;

Whom from death's sepulchral portal
Lion Mark restores immortal,
Whilst earth quakes and rocks are riven;
Him John paints with skill unstudied,
FIRST AND LAST, God in true Godhead,
Father of all earth and heaven.

Cujus lumen visuale,
Vultus anceps, leves alæ,
Rotæ stantes in quadrigâ,
Sunt in cœlo visa, prius
Quam hic esset, vel illius
Forma capax, vel auriga.

Illi scribunt Christum pati
Dolum, inde vim Pilati,
Cum coronâ spineâ:
Hic sublimis tractu pennæ
Tractat Christi jus perenne
Cum ultrici frameâ.

Pennis hujus idiotæ
Elevantur Regis rotæ,
Secus animalia.
Et cœlestes citharœdi
Se prosternunt Patris sedi
Canentes: Alleluia!

He the eyes all round these creatures,
Their swift wings, their fourfold features,
And the wheels that stand beside them,
In their might had seen in heaven,
Ere form here to them was given,
Or the charioteer to guide them.

They describe what craft Christ suffered;
Violence by Pilate offered,
With the thorn-crown, then endured:
He, borne up on soaring pinion,
Treats of Christ's supreme dominion,
And of His avenging sword.

On his wings, though uninstructed,
Rise the King's own wheels, conducted
As though on the living four;
While the heavenly harpers, kneeling
At the Father's throne, their thrilling
Alleluia's song outpour! Amen.

XXXIII.

S. JOANNES EVANGELISTA.

XXVII° DECEMBRIS.

CHRISTO laudes persolvat—hic chorus psallens—die ista,
Qua Johannes supernæ—mensæ fratrumque—est conviva !

Qui multis ex maximis—claruit miraculis—hac in vita ;
Patrem, navim, nuptias,—seque liquit, Domini—sequens vias.

Clarior hic ceteris,—supra pectus Domini—cubans cœnat ;
Huic de cruce virgini—Virgo voce Filii—est commissa.

Fervens vicit oleum,—tonsus ad ridiculum,—risit flagra.
Propter Evangelium,—subiit exilium,—ferrum, vincla.

XXXIII.

ST. JOHN THE EVANGELIST.

DECEMBER 27TH.

LET our choir upon this day,—as they lift their anthem, pay,—Christ due praises;
Day, when John became a guest—at high heaven's supernal feast—with his brethren;

Who for marvels by him done,—many and most great, was known,—whilst here living;
Father, vessel, marriage-bed—and himself he left, instead—Christ to follow.

More illustrious than the rest—lying upon Jesus' breast—at the supper;
From the Cross to this chaste one—was the Virgin by the Son—given over.

Boiling oil he overcame,—and, when shorn for scoff and shame,—mocked their scourgings;
For the Gospel's honour spent,—banishment he underwent,—torture, fetters.

Virus fidens sorbuit,—et extinctos eruit :—vir vita refloruit—et matrona ;
Aurum hic de frondibus,—gemmas de silicibus,—fractis de fragminibus—fecit firmas.

Hunc vocans visitat Christus—et hic intrat vivus foveam :—petit æthra.
Nunc te, Christe, nostra rogant—vox et vota, ipsi socia—nos per sæcla ! Amen.

He through faith did poison drain,—and the dead
revived again,—first restoring a young man,
—then a mother.
Gold from foliage fashioned he,—out of pebbles
jewelry,—and their fragments perfectly—
put together.

Christ visits him to call him home,—and he, alive
still, entereth the tomb,—thence seeks
heaven.
Now, Christ! to Thee plead voice and prayer,—
bring us to be his partners there,—through
the ages! Amen.

XXXIV.

S. JOANNES EVANGELISTA.

XXVII° DECEMBRIS.

PRÆFATIO. Trinitatem reserat aquila, summus Evangelista!

FELIX sedes gratiæ,
Summum Regem gloriæ
Videns mentis acie
Non repulsa!
Johannem deificat,
Angelis parificat,
Spiritus qui indicat
Cœli summa.

Aquæ vivæ salientis
Hic est potus recumbentis
Supra pectus Domini.
Hic exfulget miris signis,
Hic expugnat vires ignis
Et ferventis olei.

Mirantur nimia
Tormenti sævitia,

XXXIV.

ST. JOHN THE EVANGELIST.

DECEMBER 27TH.

PREFACE. John, the eagle, first of Evangelists, the
Triune God revealeth!

BLESSED resting-place of grace!
Who on heaven's great King dost gaze
With the mind's eye, face to face,
All unblinded!
For the Spirit shows God's throne
To him, deifying John,
Making him with angels one,
Heavenly-minded!

Now the water, life supplying,
As it springs up, drinks he, lying
On the bosom of the Lord:
Now he shines with many a wonder,
Now the force of fire keeps under,
And of hot oil round him poured.

Wondrous it seems to be,
That, 'mid torture's agony,

Quod martyr quis fiat,
Et pœnas non sentiat.

O martyr! O virgo!—O custos Virginis—per quam mundo gloria,
Ex quo sunt, in quo sunt,—per quem sunt omnia,—per te det suffragia!

O dilecte prae cæteris,
Christum, a quo diligeris,
Interpellans
Et exorans,
Nos ei concilia.
Tu qui rivus, duc ad fontem,
Tu qui collis, duc ad montem;
Præsta Sponsum
Ad videndum,
Virgo totus gratia.

FINIS. Sponso laus per sæcula!

Martyrdom one should gain,
And yet never feel the pain.

O martyr! O virgin!—that Virgin's guardian,—who did earth's chief Glory bear!
From Whom is, in Whom is,—through Whom is everything,—may He through thee hear our prayer!

O thou, beloved above the rest!
Ask Christ, Who loved thee far the best,
To Him pressing
Prayers addressing,
For His reconciling grace.
River! lead us to the fountain;
Hill! conduct us to the mountain;
Who endurest
Virgin purest!
Let us see the Bridegroom's face.

CONCLUSION. To the Bridegroom endless praise!

XXXV.

S. THOMAS CANTUARIUS.

XXIX° DECEMBRIS.

GAUDE, Sion, et lætare,
Voce, voto jocundare
Solemni lætitia:
Tuus Thomas trucidatur;
Pro te, Christe, immolatur,
Salutaris hostia.

Archipræsul et legatus,
Nullo tamen est elatus
Honoris fastigio;
Dispensator summi Regis,
Pro tutela sui gregis
Trusus est exilio.

Telo certans pastorali,
Ense cinctus Spiritali,
Triumphare meruit;
Hic pro Dei sui lege,
Et pro suo mori grege
Decertare studuit.

XXXV.

ST. THOMAS OF CANTERBURY.

DECEMBER 29TH.

JOY, O Sion! and rejoice thou;
With both vow and lifted voice now,
With a holy joy be glad!
For Christ's sake, assassinated,
Is thy Thomas immolated,
A most precious victim made.

Primate, legate, though created,
He was ne'er with pride elated
By his honours' lofty height;
Steward of the King of heaven,
He was into exile driven,
Since he for his flock would fight.

With the Spirit's sword girt round him,
Victory with full triumph crowned him,
As with pastoral spear he fought;
For his God's law to be fighting,
For his flock's sake death inviting,
Ever was his chiefest thought.

Tunc rectore desolatam
Et pastore viduatam
Se plangebat Canthia;
Versa vice, plausu miro,
Exultavit tanto viro
Senonensis Gallia.

Quo absente, infirmatur,
Infirmata conculcatur
Libertas Ecclesiæ;
Sic nos, pater, reliquisti,
Nec a vero recessisti
Tramite justitiæ.

Quondam cœtu curiali
Primus eras et regali
Militans palatio;
Plebis aura favorali
Et, ut mos est, temporali
Plaudebas præconio.

Consequenter es mutatus:
Præsulatu sublimatus,
Novus homo reparatus
Felici commercio,
Ex adverso ascendisti,
Et te murum objecisti:
Caput tuum obtulisti,
Christi sacrificio.

Losing then its guide and master,
And deprived thus of its pastor,
    Canterbury deeply grieved;
But then one, so justly noted,
Sens in France, with joy devoted,
    And with glad acclaim received.

In his absence sore prostrated,
And, when prostrate, violated,
    Was the Church no longer free;
So from 'mongst us thou departedst,
Father! but aside ne'er startedst
    From the path of probity.

Once, amid the courtier bevy,
Thou wast foremost of the levy
    In the palace of the king;
All the people approbation,
And the world loud acclamation,
    As its wont is, offering.

Well-timed was thy transformation;
For of thee thy consecration
By a blest reciprocation
    Made a new man happily:
Thou thine opposition endedst,
As a wall, the Church defendedst,
And thyself to death commendedst,
    Willing thus for Christ to die.

Carnis tuæ morte spreta,
Triumphalis es athleta ;
Palma tibi datur læta,
Quod testantur insueta
　　Plurima miracula.
Per te visus cæcis datur,
Claudis gressus instauratur,
Paralysis effugatur,
Vetus hostis propulsatur
　　Et peccati macula.

Cleri gemma, clare Thoma,
Motus carnis nostræ doma
　　Precum efficaciâ,
Ut, in Christo verâ vite
Radicati, vera vitæ
　　Capiamus gaudia. Amen.

Champion! who this life disdainest!
Victory in the fight thou gainest,
And the joyful palm obtainest;
Evidence of which the plainest
    All thy wonders rare afford.
To the blind their sight thou givest,
And the lame man's powers revivest;
Thou paralysis relievest,
And the old foe backward drivest,
    And transgressions' filthy horde.

Gem of priesthood, princely Thomas!
By thy prayer effectual from us
    Take our lusts, our flesh subdue;
That, in Christ, the true Vine, rooted,
We may gain, thus constituted,
    Life-joys both divine and true! Amen.

XXXVI.

S. THOMAS CANTUARIUS.

XXIX° DECEMBRIS.

PIA mater plangat Ecclesia
Quod patravit major Britannia
Factum detestabile;
Pietate movetur Francia;
Fugit cœlum, tellus et maria
Scelus exsecrabile!

Scelus, inquam, non dicendum:
Grande scelus et horrendum
Perpetravit Anglia.
Patrem suum prædamnavit,
Et in sede trucidavit
Restitutum propria.

Thomas totius Angliæ
Flos vernans, et Ecclesiæ
Specialis gloria,
In templo Cantuariæ
Pro legibus justitiæ
Fit sacerdos et hostia.

XXXVI.

ST. THOMAS OF CANTERBURY.

December 29th.

NOW let our holy Mother-Church bemoan
What was aforetime by Great Britain done ;
'Twas a deed detestable :
By pious feelings France is deeply stirred,
And in all horror from the guilt abhorred
Flee heaven and earth and seas as well !

Ah ! a crime beyond all telling,
One most hateful and repelling,
Was at England's hands then done :
She prejudged her father, newly
To his home restored, and foully
Murdered him upon his throne.

Thomas, all England's brightest flower,
The glory of the church, before
All others in exalted fame,
At Canterbury's temple door,
The laws of justice to secure,
Both sacrifice and priest became.

Inter templum et altare,
Templi super liminare
Concutitur, non frangitur;
Sed gladiis conscinditur
Velum templi medium.
Eliseus decalvatur,
Zacharias trucidatur;
Pax tradita dissolvitur
Et organum convertitur
In lamentum flentium.

Prope festum Innocentum
Innocentur ad tormentum
Pertrahitur, concutitur,
Et cerebrum effunditur
Cuspide mucronis.
Ad decoris ornamentum
Templi rubet pavimentum,
Quod sanguine respergitur,
Dum sacerdos induitur
Veste passionis.

Furor ingens debacchatur,
Sanguis justus condemnatur,
Ense caput dissecatur
In conspectu Domini:

'Twixt the temple and the altar,
On the threshold, each assaulter
Doth rudely shake, but breaks him not;
Though with their swords in twain they cut
In its midst the temple veil.
Low Elisha's bald head lieth,
Zacharias, slaughtered, dieth;
Peace, thus betrayed, dissolves away,
And the sweet organ now can play
But the tearful mourners' wail.

Upon Childermas's morrow
Is this Innocent to sorrow
Dragged forth, and blows, and tortures' pain;
Whilst, on the earth outpoured, his brain,
Lo! the sword's point bareth.
As that temple's chiefest glory,
Blushes still its pavement gory,
Which is o'ersprinkled with his blood,
As there this holy priest of God
Robes of passion weareth.

Rages wrath, with fury fevered,
Just blood is to death delivered;
With a sword his head is shivered
In the presence of the Lord:

Cum sacrabat, hic sacratur,
Immolator immolatur,
Ut virtutis relinquatur
Hoc exemplum homini.

Holocaustum medullatum,
Jam per orbem propalatum,
In odorem Deo gratum
Est pontifex oblatus;
Pro corona quæ secatur
Duplex stola præparatur,
Ubi sedes restauratur
Archiepiscopatus.

Synagoga derogat, ridet Paganismus,
Insultant idolatræ, quod Christianismus
Fœdus violaverit
Nec patri pepercerit
Christianitatis.
Rachel plorat filium, non vult consolari,
Quam in matris utero vidit trucidari;
Super cujus obitum
Dant in fletu gemitum
Mentes pietatis.

Hic est ille pontifex
Quem supernus Artifex
In cœlorum culmine

Consecrating, consecrated,
Immolating, immolated,
He to man a celebrated
    Type of virtue doth afford.

Holocaust, with marrow welling,
Known to earth's remotest dwelling,
Sacrifice to God sweet-smelling,
    This pontiff was selected;
For a crown that may be riven
Two-fold robes to him are given
On his primate's throne, in heaven
    Restored and re-erected.

Jews depreciate our fame, Pagans show derision,
Such as worship idols scoff, that our own religion
    Should to break its pledge have dared,
    Neither have that father spared,
        Over Christians reigning,
Rachel weepeth for that son, nor finds consolation,
Who thus in his mother's womb meets assassination;
    Over whose untimely end
    Holy hearts their tears expend,
        Bitterly complaining.

This man is that pontiff bright,
Whom on heaven's supremest height
    Its supernal maker, God,

Magnum stabilivit,
Postquam pertransivit
Gladios Anglorum.

Cum mori non timuit,
Sed cervicem præbuit
In suo sanguine;
Ut abhinc exivit,
Semel introivit
In sancta sanctorum.

Cujus mortem pretiosam testantur miracula,
Christe, nobis suffragetur per æterna sæcula!

Stablished in great glory,
When with swords all-gory
England's swordsmen smite him.

Since of death he felt no dread,
But surrendered up his head
To welter in his blood,
When he hence was driven
God to highest heaven
Did at once admit him.

Of his death indeed most precious mighty wonders testify;
Jesu! may he recommend us unto Thee eternally!

XXXVII.

S. THOMAS CANTUARIUS.

XXIX° DECEMBRIS.

AQUAS plenas amaritudine
Novi salis nova dulcedine,
Ollam plenam lethali gramine
Novi farris sanat pinguedine
Eliseus;
Novus vervex pro grege moritur,
Et pro matre proles occiditur;
In obscuris sol novus oritur,
In quo serus annus promittitur
Jubilæus.

Abel novum Cayn malitia,
Novum Jacob Seïr sævitia,
Novum Joseph fratrum invidia
Intercepit fraude nefariâ
His diebus.
Surrexerunt in patrem pueri,
Non materno parcentes uberi;
Thomas præsul dum datur funeri,
Novum chaos videtur ingeri
Mundi rebus.

XXXVII.

ST. THOMAS OF CANTERBURY.

DECEMBER 29TH.

A NEW Elisha bitter waters heals
With such new sweetness as new salt reveals;
The pot too, which a herb most deadly fills,
He renders harmless by the fat of meal's
New remedy.
Lo! for the flock another wether dies,
And, for the mother slain, the offspring lies:
To light our darkness a new sun doth rise,
Which the long promised year to all supplies
Of Jubilee.

'Gainst a new Abel doth Cain's malice fight;
Seir's fierceness 'gainst another Jacob's right;
Another Joseph hath his brethren's spite,
Seizing with wicked fraud, put out of sight
In these last days.
Sons 'gainst their fathers to rebel have dared,
Not having e'en their mother's bosom spared:
As Bishop Thomas to his death is snared,
Lo! a new chaos, for all earth prepared,
The eye surveys.

Sed occumbit Abel in gloria,
Jacob servat Mesopotamia,
Joseph regnat in aulâ regiâ,
Thomas noster in cœli curiâ
Coronatur.
Renovantur Anglorum gaudia,
Bethel novus fit Dorovernia,
Fit piscina propitiaria,
In qua jugis et multifaria
Salus datur.

Dilatatur Jordanis fluvius,
Fit Naäman alter et tertius,
Derivatur Siloe longius,
Cœlum pluit manna profusius
Quam solebat.
Duplicatur solaris radius;
Magnus Annæ donatur filius,
Novum vatem Herodis gladius
Trucidavit inverecundius
Quam decebat.

Trucidato non desunt præmia;
Sancto namque pro sanctimonia,
Pro sinceræ mentis constantia,
Vita, salus et lux ætherea
Condonatur.

But Abel covered with great glory falls;
Haran saves Jacob, when for help he calls;
Joseph bears rule within a monarch's walls;
Our Thomas too is crowned in the bright halls
Of highest heaven.
All Englishmen, their joys renewed, are glad,
And Canterbury, new Bethesda made,
Becomes a pool, the sinful soul to aid,
Whence at all times to all around it laid
Salvation's given.

The river Jordan wider tracts streams o'er;
Another and third Naaman seeks its shore;
Siloam's pool spreads further than before,
Whilst heaven far more profusely than of yore
Doth manna rain.
The sun's rays are with double power outpoured;
A mighty son to Hannah is secured;
Another prophet Herod's ruthless sword
With shamelessness yet more to be abhorred
Hath foully slain.

But, slaughtered thus, a full reward hath he;
For to the saint for his great sanctity,
And his pure heart's untiring constancy,
Salvation, life, and light most heavenly,
Is freely given.

Abhinc multa facit prodigia:
Lepram curat, fugat dæmonia;
Cæcis visum, claudis vestigia,
Verba mutis, ægris remedia
Imprecatur.

Vir Belial luit blasphemias,
Quas in sanctum arsit injurias;
Visu dempto, tristes exsequias
Maturando nefandas furias
Terminavit.
Vir devotus in sanctum Domini,
Zelo pravo sustractus lumini,
Sed mox datus visus acumini,
Laudes lætus divino nomini
Decantavit.

Cruces, factæ manu angelica,
Pii patris prece benefica,
Crebro pollent virtute cœlica;
Far fit humi quod paralytica
Membra sanat.
Immolentur lucernæ geminæ,
Accenduntur cœlesti lumine;
Declaratur in vasis fragmine
Locum sanctum fraudis molimine
Qui profanat.

Henceforth he works unnumbered prodigies ;
Lepers are cleansed, the devil's legion flies ;
Strength for the lame, and sight for blinded eyes,
Speech for the dumb, for sick folk remedies,
He asks of heaven.

A son of Belial blasphemies he swore,
Burning the saint to harm, atoneth for ;
The loss of sight and death did he incur,
An early death, which stopped for evermore
His wrath's fierce stream.
A man, who in the Lord's saint took delight,
And had his eyes put out by bigot spite,
But soon again recovered perfect sight,
Sang constant praises with rejoicing bright
To God's great name.

Crosses, which were by angel fingers made,
When kindly prayers this pious father prayed,
Through heavenly virtue oft great power displayed ;
And grain, that heals the limbs with palsy dead,
On earth is grown.
An offering of two lamps was made, which same
Are lighted up by a celestial flame :
The broken fragments of a vase proclaim
Who hath to some blest shrine by fraudful scheme
Dishonour done.

Calce puer qui matrem læserat
Pœnitendo calcem absciderat;
Mox, ut opem sancti petierat,
Bipedalem gressum meruerat,
Res stupenda!
Nauta potens in navi mystica,
Nostra, Thoma, laudes et cantica
Summo Regi prece gratifica
Et eidem prece magnifica
Nos commenda. Amen.

A lad, who with his foot his mother lamed,
Cut off that foot to show himself ashamed ;
Soon, when he had this saint's assistance claimed.
He walked upon two feet, as if ne'er maimed,
A wonder rare !
O seaman, who in mystic ship bear'st sway !
Our joyful praises and this grateful lay
To the great King in kindly prayer to-day,
Thomas ! commend, and us to Him, we pray,
In potent prayer ! Amen.

XXXVIII.

S. GENOVEFA.

III° JANUARII.

GENOVEFÆ solemnitas
  Solemne parit gaudium;
Cordis erumpat puritas
  In laudis sacrificium!

Felix ortus infantulæ,
Teste Germano præsule:
Quod prævidit in spiritu,
Rerum probatur exitu.

Hic ad pectus virgineum,
  Pro pudoris signaculo,
Nummum suspendit æneum,
  Crucis insignem titulo.

Genovefam divinitus
  Oblato dotat munere,
In templum Sancti Spiritus
  Sub Christi dicans fœdere.

XXXVIII.

ST. GENEVIEVE.

JANUARY 3RD.

GENEVIEVE a holy mirth
  Brings forth upon her holy day;
Then let the chastened heart break forth,
  The sacrifice of praise to pay !

Blest was that infant's birth of yore,
As Bishop Germain witness bore,
And what in spirit he foreknew
The issue of events proves true.

Upon the virgin's bosom laid,
  To mark her spotless chastity,
A medal, that of bronze was made,
  Stamped with a cross suspendeth he.

Genevieve he then endows
  With gifts that heaven-sent power can boast,
And consecrates through Christian vows
  A temple for the Holy Ghost.

Insontem manu feriens,
  Mater privatur lumine;
Matri virgo compatiens
  Lucis dat usum pristinæ.

Genovefa magnanimis
  Carnem frangit jejunio,
Terramque rigans lacrymis,
  Jugi gaudet martyrio.

Cœlesti duce prævio,
  Cœlos lustrat et tartara,
Civesque precum studio
  Servat a gente barbara.

Divino diu munere
  Sitim levat artificum;
Confractum casu miseræ
  Matri resignat unicum.

Ad primam precem virginis
  Contremiscunt dæmonia;
Pax datur energuminis,
  Spes ægris, reis venia.

In ejus manus cerei
  Reaccenduntur cœlitus;
Per hanc in sinus alvei
  Redit amnis coercitus.

For striking at the guileless maid
  Her mother's eyes lose all their light;
The virgin, for her mother sad,
  Restores to them their former sight.

Genevieve, the great-souled, wears
  Her fleshly frame by fasts away,
And joys, bedewing earth with tears,
  In martyrdom from day to day.

'Neath angel guidance she surveys
  The heavens above and hell below;
And saves, so fervently she prays,
  The people from a barbarous foe.

Long doth she with unearthly power
  Some workmen's thirst alleviate;
And at a mother's tears restore
  Her only son, struck down by fate.

At the pure maiden's earliest prayer
  Trembles and quakes all Satan's race;
While rest and peace demoniacs share,
  The sickly hope, the guilty grace.

Some waxen tapers in her hand
  With heaven-sent flame are made to burn;
Its waters too at her command
  Back to a river's bed return.

Ignem sacrum refrigerat,
  Post mortem vivens meritis,
Quæ prius in se vicerat
  Æstus interni fomitis.

Morti, morbis, dæmonibus,
  Et elementis imperat :
Sic Genovefa precibus
  Naturæ leges superat.

Operatur in parvulis
  Christi virtus magnalia :
Christo, pro tot miraculis,
  Laus frequens, jugis gloria ! Amen.

She by her merits,—living still
  When dead,—cools down "the Ardents'" fire,
Who in herself before could quell
  The flames within of hot desire.

Disease, death, powers of the air,
  And elements, all own her sway;
So Genevieve by force of prayer
  Makes Nature's laws her will obey.

In very babes Christ's power alone
  Works mighty deeds effectually:
To Christ for such great wonders done
  All praise and endless glory be! Amen.

XXXIX.

S. AGNES.

XXI° JANUARII.

ANIMEMUR ad agonem,
Recolentes passionem
Gloriosæ virginis:
Contrectantes sacrum florem,
Respiremus ad odorem
Respersæ dulcedinis.

Pulchra, prudens et illustris,
Jam duobus Agnes lustris
Addebat triennium:
Proles amat hanc præfecti,
Sed ad ejus virgo flecti
Respuit arbitrium.

Mira vis fidei,
Mira virginitas,
Mira virginei
Cordis integritas!

XXXIX.

ST. AGNES.

JANUARY 21ST.

AS we tell once more the fashion
Of this glorious virgin's passion,
Be we kindled to the fight:
As we touch the sacred flower,
Let us breathe the scents that shower
From its sweetness' full delight!

Beautiful and wise and noble,
Agnes now had to the double
Of five years an added three:
Much the prefect's first-born loves her,
But to maiden scorn he moves her,
Not submission to his plea.

Wonderful power of faith,
Wondrous virginity,
Wonderful virtue hath
Virgin hearts' constancy!

Sic Dei Filius,
Nutu mirabili,
Se mirabilius
Prodit in fragili.

Languet amans, cubat lecto,
Languor notus fit præfecto;
Maturat remedia.
Offert multa, spondet plura,
Periturus peritura,
Sed vilescunt omnia.

Nudam prostituit
Præses flagitiis,
Quam Christus induit
Comarum fimbriis
Stolaque cœlesti.
Cœlestis nuntius
Assistit propius;
Cella libidinis
Fit locus luminis:
Turbantur incesti.

Cæcus amans indignatur,
Et irrumpens præfocatur
A maligno spiritu.
Luget pater, lugent cuncti,
Roma flevit pro defuncti
Juvenis interitu.

So did the Son of God
Come of His wondrous will,
And in frail flesh abode;
Which is more wondrous still!

Sick, to bed the lover goeth:
When the cause the prefect knoweth,
Quickly seeks he for a cure:
Much now, vowing more, he proffers,—
Short-lived offerer, short-lived offers!—
But his gifts are all too poor.

Her doth the prefect, bare,
To outrage vile expose,
But a thick fringe of hair
Christ round her body throws,
And a robe heaven-whitened.
One of the angel-race
Beside her takes his place;
The den of lust that night
Becomes the abode of light,
And the lewd are frightened.

Her blind lover, most indignant,
Rushes in, and a malignant
Spirit robs him of life-breath.
Weeps his father, all are crying,
Rome bewailed a young man dying
By so terrible a death.

Suscitatur ab Agnete;
Turba fremit indiscrete;
    Rogum parant virgini:
Rogus ardens reos urit,
In furentes flamma furit,
    Dans honorem numini.

Grates agens Salvatori,
Guttur offert hæc lictori;
Nec ad horam timet mori,
    Puritatis conscia.
Agnes, Agni salutaris
Stans ad dextram gloriaris,
Et parentes consolaris,
    Invitans ad gaudia.

Ne te flerent ut defunctam,
Jam cœlesti Sponso junctam,
His, sub agni forma, suam
Revelavit atque tuam
    Virginalem gloriam;
Nos ab Agno salutari
Non permitte separari,
Cui te totam consecrasti,
Cujus ope tu curasti
    Nobilem Constantiam.

Vas electum, vas honoris,
Incorrupti flos odoris,

He is raised by Agnes' pleading;
But the crowd,—blind rage misleading !—
For the maid prepare the stake :
Its bright blaze the guilty burneth ;
'Gainst the fierce the fierce flame turneth
For the Most High's honour's sake.

To the Saviour thanks she proffers,
To the lictor her throat offers ;
Neither fears she when she suffers,
Conscious of her purity.
Agnes ! thou, thy crown receiving,
At the saving Lamb's side living,
Comfort to thy parents giving,
Bidd'st them mount to joys on high !

Lest they mourn, as dead and buried,
One, to Spouse divine now married,
In a lamb's shape, Christ the story
Of His own and of thy glory
Set before them, spotless maid !
Suffer not our separation
From that Lamb, our One salvation ;
Unto Whom devoted wholly,
Thou didst noble Constance throughly
Heal of sickness by His aid.

Vessel, glorious and elected !
Flower, with scent by naught affected !

Angelorum grata choris,
Honestatis et pudoris
    Forman præbes sæculo.
Palma fruens triumphali,
Flore vernans virginali,
Nos indignos speciali,
Fac sanctorum generali
    Vel subscribi titulo. Amen.

By the angelic choirs respected!
Thou art as the type erected
    Of a maiden's spotless fame.
Off the palm of victory bearing,
Still thy virgin blossom wearing,
Grant we may, unfit appearing
For a special title, share in,
    With the saints, their general name! Amen.

NOTES.

NOTES.

SEQUENCE I.

1. "Christus natus non est per conditionem sed per potestatem."—*August.* "De Trinit." iii. 26.

7. "So in the Greek Anthology, ὁ ἀχώρητος χωρεῖται."—*Trench*, ad loc., "Sacred Latin Poetry," 3rd edit. p. 113.

19-20. Cf. Luke, ii. 10, 13; Matth. iv. 11; Luke xxii. 43; Matth. xxviii. 2.

31, 32. Cf. Matth. xxvii. 34; Ps. lxix. 21.

33-36. Cf. Adam's Sequence on the Circumcision, page 46 in this volume, where he enlarges on the good Samaritan as the type of Christ, lines 7-14.

37 et ss. Cf. 2 Kings iv. 7-37; and on Elisha as a type of Christ, *Bernard,* "In Cant. Serm. 15, 16."

41. The "Giants" of Gen. vi. 4, according to the interpretation of the early Church, *Geminæ substantiæ;* the "sons of God" who begat them, (ver. 2,) being angels, who formed unions with the "daughters of men." Cf. Ps. xix. 5, *Trench.* The application of this to our Lord as God and man is obvious, and is used more than once by St. Ambrose. Cf. his hymn, "Veni, Redemptor gentium."

45. *Mone*, vol. ii., page 86, reads "Vicit."

47, 48. "There is allusion here to that interpretation of the parable of the pieces of silver (Luke xv. 8-10) which makes the nine which were not lost to be the nine ranks of angels who stood in their first obedience, and the one lost to be the race of mankind."—*Trench*, ad loc.

49. *Meta Vatum*. "Because with Christ's birth the prophets of the O. T. ceased."—*Mone*, "Hymni Lat. Med. Ævi," vol. ii. p. 87.

SEQUENCE II.

1, 2. Cf. Luke ii. 13, 14: "And suddenly there was with the angels a multitude of the heavenly host, praising God, and saying, 'Glory to God in the highest, on earth peace, goodwill towards men!'"

11, 12. Cf. Hebrews iv. 15: "For we have not an High-Priest, which cannot be touched with the feeling of our infirmities; but was in all points tempted like as we are, yet without sin."

17. Vid. note on Sequence lxxiv. 45-47. Cf. Daniel ii. 34.

20, 22. Cf. Isaiah vii. 14; Matth. i. 18, 22, 23; Luke i. 27.

25. Cf. Isaiah xi. 1, 2; Romans xv. 12: "The stem is the Virgin, the flower Jesus. One can refer to numberless 'Jesse Trees' which have been carved over the doorways and on the walls of our cathedrals. Liturgical poetry often took its inspiration from the passage in Isaiah. A response in verse by Fulbert de Chartres, music for which was composed by the pious King Robert, was especially popular in the middle ages.

> 'Stirps Jesse virgam produxit virgaque florem,
> Et super hunc florem requiescit spiritus almus,
> Virgo Dei genetrix virga est, flos Filius ejus,
> Et super hunc florem requiescit spiritus almus.'"

Gautier, ad loc.

Sequence III.

51. Gautier says here, "Aaron's rod that blossomed is the emblem of the Virgin Mary, who bore a child without losing her virginity, and gave to the world that Jesus *jure flori comparatus.*"

52. "The fleece of Gideon, which, on a soil perfectly dry, was saturated with dew, is the type of Mary, who became a mother without experience of carnal intercourse." —*Gautier*, ad loc.

59. *Stella Maris* is the exact translation of the name of *Mary* according to St. Jerome.

Sequence IV.

1, 2, 3. Cf. Luke i. 79: "To give light to them that sit in darkness and in the shadow of death."

Sequence V.

11, 12. "The Virgin Mary had no model in the past, *exemplar;* nor can she in the future find a faithful likeness, *exemplum:*

Gaudia Matris habens cum virginitatis honore,
Nec primam similem visa est nec habere sequentem."

Sedulius, "Carmen Paschale," ii. 67, 68.

Gautier, ad loc.

Vid. also the "Great Antiphon" in the *Sarum Breviary* for December 23rd, "O Virgo Virginum."

14. Cf. Genesis iii. 2.

Sequence VI.

7-12. "Nothing is more common in liturgical poetry than the comparison of Eve with Mary, *The New Eve.*"—*Gautier*, ad loc.

It begins very early indeed, being found in *St. Irenæus*, "Adv. Hær," v. 19.

17-22. Cf. Psalm xix. 5, and note on Sequence i. line 41 *ante.*

SEQUENCE VII.

29, 30. Cf. Numbers xvii. 8.

32. Cf. Judges vi. 37 et seq.

45-53. "These three stanzas are devoted to the double symbolism of the almond or the nut. The nut is first *in itself* the representation of Jesus Christ; its bitter hull is the anguish of the cross *circa carnem;* the shell of the nut is the body of our Lord, and the fruit the Godhead clothed with flesh, the sweetness of Christ. By its properties moreover the nut is the representation of Christ; it offers us three benefits, *unction, light, nourishment.* Is not Christ the light of the blind, the unction of the sick, the food of the faithful in the Eucharist?"—*Gautier,* ad loc.

SEQUENCE VIII.

5, 6. Cf. Luke xv. 8. "The lost piece of silver" symbolizes man after the fall. "The lighted candle" Christ, the light of the world, sent to seek "that which was lost."

7-14. Cf. Luke x. 30-37. The good Samaritan symbolizes Christ; the man that fell among thieves mankind; the oil and wine the sacraments; the two pence the two testaments.

15, 16. Cf. Judges vi. 37 et seq.

18, 26. A reference to the symbolic character of the number *eight,* which makes it so often the sign of finality: that finality being a complete restoration and happy summing up of all.

The hymnist asks in lines 25, 26, that he and others may have their share in the blessings of that completing age and epoch of the church.

SEQUENCE IX.

11. Cf. 1 Cor. xi. 3: "The head of every man is Christ."

12. Cf. 1 Cor. vi. 15, and xii. 27: "Now ye are the body of Christ, and members in particular."

13. Cf. 1 Cor. v. 7: "Christ our Passover is sacrificed for us."

16. Cf. 1 Peter v. 8, Vulgate, "Adversarius noster, tanquam leo rugiens, circuit, quærens quem devoret."

18, 19. Cf. Judges xiv. 6.

20-23. Cf. 1 Sam. xvii. 34-36. *Fortibus manibus* is the translation of the word "David."

27. *Sol eorum.* "This etymology of Samson's name is derived from Jerome, who ('De Nom. Heb.') explains Samson: '*Sol eorum*, vel *solis fortitudo*,—*their* light, or the light of them that are His.' . . . . They may have been right in seeing *shemesh* or 'the sun' in Samson's name; but '*sol eorum*' is of course a mistake."—*Trench*, ad loc.

"Samson"="Solar" according to modern scholars.

31. Cf. Numb. xiii. 23, 24. The "one cluster of grapes" and the "staff" upon which it was borne, are constantly, as noted by Archbishop Trench, counted among the O. T. types of Christ and His cross. The archbishop quotes Hugh of St. Victor, *Inst. Mor.* i. 4, August., Enarr. in Ps. viii. 1, and the following lines from Pet. de Riga to illustrate this fact:

> In ligno botrus est pendens, in cruce Christus;
> Profluit hinc vinum, profluit inde salus.
> Ejicitur prælo de botro gratia vini;
> Prælo pressa crucis sanguis et unda fluit.
> *Trench*, "Sacred Lat. Poetry," pp. 164, 165.

36-38. *Saccus siccus.* Cf. Ps. xxx. 11, E. V.; xxix. 12, Vulgate. "The sackcloth is here the flesh of Christ; the 'royal uses' its immortality of glory after His death."—*Neale*, "Mediæval Hymns," in a note ad loc., page 117.

41. *Dei.* Trench considers *rei* a far better reading, and it is

used in the missals of Clugny and Paris. I have ventured, however, to retain Gautier's reading of *dei*, as occurring in the larger number of both MSS. and printed editions of this hymn.

43. "The poet with only the Vulgate before him, in which he found (Gen. iv. 15) 'Posuitque Dominus Cain signum,' Cain being undeclined, understood the passage thus:—'The Lord set Cain for a sign,' instead of 'The Lord set a sign upon Cain.'"—*Trench's* note, ad loc.

44-47. Cf. Psalm cxviii. 22: "The stone which the builders refused is become the head-stone in the corner;" Isaiah xxviii. 16; Mark xii. 10; Luke xx. 17; Matth. xxi. 42; Acts iv. 11; Ephes. ii. 20; 1 Peter ii. 6, 7.

SEQUENCE X.

10. Cf. John xii. 36: "While ye have the light, believe in the light, that ye may be the children of light."

25, 26. Cf. Exodus xii. 5: "Your lamb shall be *without blemish*."

SEQUENCE XI.

25-28. "The reference is to the question, put by God to Job, 'Canst thou draw out Leviathan with a hook?'—Job xli. 1, 2. But what man was unable to do, that Christ could and did effect on the true Leviathan, Satan. Thus, according to the Fathers, our Lord's humanity was the bait, His Divinity the hook; Satan, unconsciously swallowing the one, was destroyed by the other. Thus . . . . St. Hildebert in his epigrams, if we may so call them, named 'The Moral Interpretation of Scripture:'—

'Fisher the Father is; this world the sea;
Christ's flesh the bait, the hook His Deity,
The line His generation. Satan took
The offered bait, and perished by the hook.'"

Neale's "Med. Hymns," pp. 122, 123.

43, 44. "At Easter the song of 'Alleluia' begins again, which the church puts away through the whole of Lent." —*Gautier,* ad loc.

SEQUENCE XII.

31. Cf. Rev. v. 5; Amos iii. 8.

44. A reference to the *double* alleluias in the responses to the Lessons and at the close of an Office, peculiar in several rites to Easter-tide.

SEQUENCE XIII.

23. Some MSS., *e.g.*, the Paris Missal, read "fallitur" for "tollitur."

27. Cf. John xiv. 30: "The prince of this world cometh, and hath *nothing* in me."

34. Cf. Gen. iii. 24: "He placed at the east of the Garden of Eden cherubims and a flaming sword, *which turned every way* to keep the way of the Tree of Life."

SEQUENCE XIV.

1, 2. Cf. 1 Cor. v. 7, 8: "Purge out therefore the old leaven, . . let us keep the feast not with the old leaven . . but with the unleavened bread of sincerity and truth"; Exod. xii. 19.

4-6. Cf. Exod. xii. 41, 42.

12. Cf. Exod. i. 14; v. 12.

16. Cf. Psalm cxviii. 24.

19-21. Cf. Heb. x. 1; Col. ii. 17; Rom. x. 4; 2 Cor. i. 20.

25. Cf. Gen. xxi. 6. St. Hildebert, following the Fathers, says, "Isaac, whose name by interpretation is *laughter*, signifies Christ. For Christ is the joy of men and angels."—*Neale*, "Med. Hymns," page 122.

"The use of *forma* for *figura*, τύπος, is frequent."—*Trench*, "Sacred Latin Poetry," p. 168.

31 et seq. Cf. Exodus vii. 10-12.

38. Cf. Job xl. 20, 21, Vulgate; xli. 1, 2, E. V. Vid. Note to Sequence xi. 25-28.

39. Cf. Isaiah xi. 8. "Regulus, the diminutive of 'rex,' answers to 'basilisk,' a name we give to a serpent with crown-like, and so *kingly* marks upon its head."—*Trench*, ad loc.

43-45. Cf. 2 Kings ii. 23-25.

46. "Arreptitius" = *arreptus furore*. Cf. 1 Sam. xxi. 14. St. Augustine uses the word in his "De Civ. Dei," ii. 4. The same author in another work expounds the mystery of David's supposed madness, and of the prophecy which was therein of Christ, of whom the people said, "He is mad and hath a devil." David's escape from the presence of Achish represents to him Christ's escape at His resurrection from the Jews. *Enarr. I. in Ps.* xxxiii. Cf. *Trench*, ad loc.

47, 48. Cf. Lev. xvi. 22; xiv. 49-53.

49. Cf. Judges xvi. 2, 3.

58. "The legend, frequent in the middle ages, that the lion's whelps were born dead, and first roused to life on the third day by the roar of their sire, was often contemplated as a natural type of the Resurrection."—*Trench*, "Sacred Latin Poetry," note, page 70.

65. Cf. Canticles i. 14: "My beloved is unto me as a cluster of camphire in the vineyards of En-gedi."

Botrus cypri = *Cyprus grape*, used in this passage in the Vulgate, is an error from following the Septuagint, "βοτρὺς τῆς κύπρου," where the last word does not mean the island *Cyprus*, but merely copies the Hebrew "kopher" = camphor-plant, and *botrus* means only *cluster*.

72. Cf. Matthew xxvii. 52.

73, 74. Cf. Psalm xxx. 5.

SEQUENCE XVI.

10-12. Cf. Deut. xxxii. 13: "Honey out of the rock and oil out of the flinty rock."

25. Cf. Lev. xviii. 16, 17. The poet alludes probably to the mediæval interpretation of the *two* loaves offered as first-fruits at the end of harvest, as typifying that the first-fruits of the Christian Church on the Day of Pentecost should be two-fold, viz.: Jews and Gentiles.

31, 32. Cf. Matthew ix. 17: *Utres novi*: "sunt homines per gratiam innovati." *Utres vetusti*: "sunt homines peccatores veterem hominem cum actibus suis imitantes." *Sunt capaces novi musti:* "In novos [utres] vinum ponendum est novum scilicet Spiritus Sanctus qui vinum novum dicitur ab effectu, etc." *Petrus Cantor.*, "Spicilegium Solesmense," ii. 462. Quoted by Gautier, ad loc.

33, 34. Cf. 2 Kings iv. 1-7.

53, 54. Cf. Gen. i. 2. As the Spirit moved over the face of the waters at the Creation, so does it, the poet suggests, over the waters of baptism.

SEQUENCE XVII.

1. *Ab utroque.* Adam here emphasizes a protest against the heresy of the Greek Church as to the procession of the Holy Ghost from the Father alone.

SEQUENCE XVIII.

3. Gautier reads *reformet* for *illustret.* I have preferred the latter, as the reading adopted by Archbishop Trench and Daniel.

7-28. "These stanzas are in the true spirit of St. Paul and St. Augustine, and hardly to be understood fully without reference to the writings of the latter, above all to his anti-Pelagian tracts, wherein he constantly contrasts, as Adam does here, the killing letter of the old, and the quickening spirit of the new, covenant."—*Trench*, ad loc.

19, 20. Cf. Exodus xix. 16, Vulgate: "Ecce cœperunt audiri tonitrua ac micare fulgura, et nubes densissima operire montem, clangorque buccinæ vehementius perstrepebat."

21, 22. Cf. Exodus xx. 18, Vulgate: "Cunctus autem populus videbat voces et lampades, et sonitum buccinæ, montemque fumantem: et perterriti ac pavore concussi steterunt procul."

30 et seq. Cf. Acts ii.

40. "The poet sees in the Jewish year of Jubilee—the year of restitution and restoration—a type of that great epoch of re-creation and restoration that began at Pentecost."—*Trench*, ad loc. Cf. Lev. xxv.

47, 48. *Vel dimittens vel mutatus*: "These etymologies of *Jubilee* have long been given up."—*Trench*, ad loc.

Dr. Littledale, in writing to me on this point, says: "It is not quite correct to say that the etymology *dimittens* has long been given up. There is a good deal to be said for it, and the verb which yields the meaning, יבל, agrees, except in vocal points, with that which is accepted by most modern critics, meaning to "flow impetuously," and held to refer to the flowing from the trumpets. But there is quite as much to be said for the earlier view, supported as it is by Josephus,"—who in "Ant.," iii. 12, 3, makes it mean "liberty." Modern critics, following Kranold, interpret the word as "Id quod magno strepitu fluit "=*a rushing, penetrating sound.* Cf. *Smith's* "Dict. of the Bible," vol. i. p. 1151.

Sequence XIX.

41 et seq. This stanza is unfinished in the MSS.

58. This repetition of line 50 is probably a clerical error of the transcriber, which cannot unfortunately be corrected now.

Sequence XX.

21-28. Vide note on Sequence xvi. 53, 54, *ante.*

23. Cf. Gen. i. 2, Vulgate: "Et Spiritus Dei *ferebatur* super aquas."

35. Cf. Isaiah iv. 1.

37. The word *forma* is one of the most difficult in mediæval philosophy, but the meaning it mostly bore at the date of Adam of St. Victor was that property which made anything to be a *species* of its *genus.* Thus *essence* or *kind* will come near to its intention. Here Adam's notion would seem to be that the Holy Spirit is the *anima mundi.* I have used the word "type" in this stanza, not in its meaning of *allegory* or *similitude*, but as representing any *form* or *species* of being or idea.

Sequence XXII.

7, 8. "*Relative* significat vox quæ relationem significat, ut vox *Pater*: importat enim relationem ad Filium. *Substantive* autem vox quæ significat aliquid per se subsistens absque ullo respectu ad aliud, ut vox *Deus.*" (*Lexicon quo veterum philosophorum locutiones explicantur*, Tornaci. Casterman, 1849.)

"Gautier explains that the Latin adverb 'relative' is used here with special reference to the relation subsisting between the divine persons of the Blessed Trinity; also that the word 'substantive' signifies that which subsists without reference to any other, as doth God."—D. T. Morgan's "Hymns, &c., of the Latin Church," note, page 151.

SEQUENCE XXIII.

1, 2. Cf. Ps. lxxxiv. 1, 2, in our Bibles. The words of the Vulgate are: "Quam dilecta tabernacula tua, Domine virtutum! Concupiscit et deficit anima mea in atria Domini." This Psalm, Gautier says, is chanted whilst the bishop is sprinkling the proposed site of a church with holy water. *Tabernaculum* signifies "temple;" but the material temple is here only the representation of the spiritual temple, where God is worshipped "in spirit and in truth"—the Church. It is then of the Church, as the congregation of the faithful, that Adam speaks throughout this sequence, without doubt one of the most difficult, and perhaps the most figurative, of all of his. Cf. *Gautier*, ad loc.

3-6. Cf. Matthew vii. 24, 25; Ephes. ii. 20; Rev. xxi. 14.

10-12. Cf. Gen. ii. 21, 22. As woman was formed out of a rib taken from Adam's side whilst he slept, so the sacraments flowed from the side of Christ, when pierced by the spear, during His sleep of death upon the Cross. *Umbra*, in line 10, = the Old Testament.

13-15. Cf. Gen. vii. The ark typifies the Church on earth, riding in safety over the floods of the world's wickedness. Noah is the type of Christ.

16-18. Cf. Gen. xviii. 12, 13. Sarah typifies the Church on earth, and Isaac Christ. On *gaudium*, vide note to Hymn xiv., line 25, ante.

20. Cf. Gen. xxiv. 17-20. "According to the mediæval allegory,—Isaac is Christ; Rebecca the Gentile Church; Eliezer the Apostles and Doctors whom He sent to betroth that Church to Himself; the servant's thirst, their ardour for souls, satisfied by the obedience of the Gentile converts, as Eliezer's by the pitcher of Rebecca."—*Neale*, "Mediæval Hymns," page 150.

23. Cf. Gen. xxiv. 22. "As Rebecca puts on the bracelets and ear-rings which Isaac sent her, so the Gentile Church adorns herself for her Lord; but with ornaments of His giving."—*Trench*, ad loc.

25-27. Cf. Gen. xxvii. 5. "Esau going away to hunt here represents the Jew, who while wandering in search of the letter of the Scriptures, and careless about the spirit, lost the blessing, which Jacob obtained."—*Neale*, "Mediæval Hymns," p. 150.

28, 29. Cf. Gen. xxix., xxx. "Leah and Rachel typify here the Synagogue and the Church—Leah the Synagogue, *lippa*, unable to see Christ, the true end of the law; but Rachel, or the Church, *videns*, seeing the things that belong unto her peace."—*Trench*, ad loc.

31. Cf. Gen. xxxviii. 14. "Tamar is the Gentile Church; the garment, in which she sat by the wayside, confession of sins; her becoming the mother of twins by Judah, while he was ignorant who she was, is explained of that text,—'A people that have not known me shall serve me.'—Psalm xviii. 48."—*Neale*, "Mediæval Hymns," p. 151.

34-36. Cf. Exod. ii. "The Nile is the world, because it flows through Egypt, the land of darkness. Moses is the natural state of man; the Ark his vain endeavour to work out a righteousness of his own; Pharaoh's daughter the grace of God, which finally makes him by adoption a son of the true King."—*Neale*, "Med. Hymns," p. 151.

37-39. Cf. Exod. xii. 5; 1 Cor. v. 7.

40-42. "In mari rubro submersus est Pharao et principes ejus; et in baptismo liberamur a potestate diaboli et principum ejus."—*Hugh of St. Victor.*

44-46. *Ædis ornamenta.* "The candlestick, altar of incense, table of shew-bread, and the like. The poet would say, 'Here, in the tabernacle which the Lord hath pitched, are these in their truth, and not, as in that of old, the mere figures of the true,'—Hebrews ix."—*Trench*, ad loc.

The pot is Christ's Manhood; the manna His Godhead; the Ten Commandments typify the new law that Christ brought from heaven, and committed to the care of the Church = the Ark of the covenant.

47, 48. *Poderis.* Cf. Exod. xxviii. 4 and 31. "The poet would say, 'Here, in the Church, are the realities which the *garments* of the high-priest, *indumenta*, and the robe, *poderis*, the chief among them, did but foreshow." —*Trench*, ad loc.

Hic sunt ædis ornamenta. Symbolical meanings were attached to the ornaments of the Temple by Mediæval writers, *e.g.*, the table of shew-bread signified Holy Scripture; its "crown of gold round about," preaching; its four rings, the four Gospels; the staves, preachers; and the twelve loaves, the Apostles' doctrine, and so on. Cf. *Hugh of St. Victor's* "Allegories on *Numbers*," chaps. xi., xii.

Hic Aaron indumenta. Each of the High Priest's vestments also had mystic meaning in Mediæval symbolism; according to the same authority,—"Allegories on *Exodus*," chap. xv., when commenting on Exod. ii. 28,—the breastplate was wisdom and discretion; the ephod, endurance; the robe, well-doing; the girdle, preparation therefor; the gold plate—upon the front of the mitre—confession of the faith; the golden bell, the preaching of it, &c.

49-54. Cf. 2 Samuel xi. 26, 27; Ps. xlv. 9. "Uriah sets forth the Jews; Bathsheba, the true Church; David represents Christ. . . The symbolical interpretation of the history is very well given by Hildebert:

"Bersabee lex est; rex David; Christus Urias;
Judæo regi nuda puella placet.
Nuda placet Christo lex non vestita figuris;
Aufert Judæis hanc, sociatque sibi.

"Vir non vult intrare domum, nec spiritualem
Intellectum plebs Israel ingreditur.
Scripta gerit, per scripta perit deceptus Urias;
Sic et Judæus scripta sequendo perit."
Neale, "Med. Hymns," p. 152.

55. "The coming of the Queen of the South—Matthew xii. 24—to hear the wisdom of Solomon—1 Kings x.—was a favourite type of the coming of the Gentile world to hear the wisdom of a greater than Solomon."—*Trench*, ad loc.

58. Cf. Cant. i. 5; 2 Cor. iv. 7. The Church "hath her treasure in earthen vessels."

60. Cf. Cant. iii. 6. The Church, as the bride, is likened to "a pillar of smoke perfumed with myrrh and frankincense, with all powders of the merchant."

64-66. "*Nuptiæ* sunt Christi et Ecclesiæ; *dilectus* est Christus; *lectus* unitas ecclesiæ."—*S. Melito.*

67-69. "According to the Mediæval allegory . . . the trumpets, as usually employed in the Jewish feasts, are the harsher Law; the sweeter psaltery is the gentler teaching of the Gospel."—*Neale*, "Med. Hymns," p. 152.

SEQUENCE XXIV.

7 et seq. Cf. 1 Kings vi., vii.; 2 Chron. iii. iv.

33-35. Each of the perfumes named is symbolic, according to Mediæval interpretation, *e.g.*, *cinnamon* stands for the "odour of sanctity;" *myrrh*, from its bitterness, signifies "the mortification of the flesh;" *stacte*, or myrrh-oil, what results from such mortification; *cassia*, being purgative, represents confession; or the three perfumes may be taken as signifying respectively penitence, mortification, and pardon.

SEQUENCE XXV.

4. Cf. Gen. xxviii. 12. The Church is the ladder, which, like Jacob's, stretches from earth to heaven, by which man may reach the last and God visits the first.

11, 12. *Vetusta historia* is the Old Testament; *moderna pagina*, the New.

13, 14. Cf. Psalm cxxxii. 13, 14.

24. Cf. Cant. ii. 13.

25. Cf. Cant. ii. 10.

26. Cf. Cant. vi. 10.

27, 28. Cf. Cant. vii. 5.

29. Cf. Cant. iv. 1.

30. Cf. Cant. iv. 3.

31. Cf. Cant. vii. 4.

32. Cf. Cant. iv. 11.

SEQUENCE XXVI.

1. "Jerusalem" and "Sion" are used figuratively to denote the Church Triumphant and the Church Militant.

9-12. Reference probably is here made to Cant. vi. 9; possibly to the forty-fifth Psalm, and *reginis* in the twelfth line would in that case represent the "kings' daughters" in the ninth verse of the Psalm. Mone (i. 326) sees a reference in the expression to the Queen of Sheba.

17-24. "Hæc enim Ecclesia jam in primo homine præfigurata est; nam sicut ex Adæ latere fabricata est Eva, ita et ex corpore Christi et vulnere redempta crevit Ecclesia."—*Leçons du bréviaire de Langres pour le Jour de la Dédicace.* Vide note on Sequence xxiii. 10-12.

30. Cf. Cant. vi. 9, Vulgate: "Pulchra ut luna, electa ut sol."

31, 32. Cf. Cant. vi. 3 and 9, Vulgate: "Pulchra es, amica mea, et decora sicut Jerusalem: terribilis *ut castrorum acies ordinata.*"

37. As the Jordan of old was parted in the midst to make a pathway by which the ark of the covenant and the Israelites might pass through it, so the ranks of the Gentile world have opened out to admit the new dispensation of Christ.

38-40. The Queen of Sheba here represents the Church coming to hear the wisdom of one greater than Solomon.

47, 48. Cf. Rev. xix. 7.

SEQUENCE XXVII.

St. Andrew, so runs the legend, who preached the Gospel in Thrace and Scythia, having been arrested by Ægeas, the proconsul at Patras in Achaia, was first cast into prison, then cruelly scourged, and at last crucified. During the two days that he lived upon the cross he never ceased instructing the people; and having prayed to our Lord not to suffer him to be taken down from the cross, he was surrounded by a great light from heaven, and, after it presently disappeared, departed this life.

7 et seq. Cf. John i. 36, 37, 40-42.

13. Cf. Matthew iv. 18 et seq.

37. Vide the hymn, "Salve, tropæum gloriæ," which Archbishop Trench gives in his "Sacred Latin Poetry," p. 219. It is there attributed to the Venerable Bede, and its subject is "St. Andrew addressing the Cross."

SEQUENCE XXVIII.

St. Nicholas belongs to the fourth century of the Christian era, and was a native of the city of Patara, in Lycia, in Asia Minor. So strong were his devotional tendencies, even from infancy, that the legend asserts that he refused to suck the breast on Wednesdays and Fridays, the fast-days appointed by the Church. He afterwards became Archbishop of Myra, the capital of

Lycia. Whilst he was still resident at Patara, a nobleman in that town, who had three daughters, had sunk to such depths of poverty, as to be on the point of selling their persons for prostitution, as the only means of preserving them from starvation. St. Nicholas, who had inherited a large fortune, no sooner heard of this unfortunate family, than he resolved to save it from the degradation with which it was threatened. As he proceeded secretly to the nobleman's house at night, debating how he might best accomplish his object, the moon shone out from behind a cloud, and showed him an open window into which he threw a purse of gold. This fell at the nobleman's feet, and enabled him to portion his eldest daughter. A second nocturnal visit was paid to the house by the saint, and a similar present bestowed, which procured a dowry for the second daughter. But the father was now determined to discover his mysterious benefactor, and with that view set himself to watch. On St. Nicholas approaching and preparing to throw in a purse of money for the third daughter, the nobleman caught hold of the skirt of his robe, and threw himself at his feet, exclaiming, "O Nicholas! servant of God! why seek to hide thyself?" But the saint made him promise that he would inform no one of this seasonable act of benevolence.

On another occasion he is said to have personally appeared to and saved some sailors, who had invoked his assistance during a storm.

He was buried at Myra, but during the eleventh century some merchants of Bari, on the Adriatic, carried off his bones to Italy. On the day they landed, May 9th, 1087, at Bari, we are told that thirty persons were cured of various distempers, and since that time his tomb has been famous for pilgrimages.

The above facts are taken, with very little alteration, from a long account of this saint in Chambers's "Book of

Days," and include most of the wonders dwelt upon in this sequence. Vol. ii. pp. 661, 662.

SEQUENCE XXIX.

15. *Lucis adversarii.* Cf. John viii. 12; i. 9.
16. Cf. Acts vi. 9, 13.
18. Cf. Luke iii. 7.
24. Cf. Rev. ii. 9.
31. Cf. 1 Peter i. 4.
37-48. Cf. Acts vii. 55, 56.
49-54. Cf. Acts vii. 57, 58.
55-60. Cf. Acts vii. 59, 60.
63-66. Cf. St. Augustine's "Civitas Dei," lib. xxii.
66-70. Cf. Acts. viii. 2: "*συνεκόμισαν δὲ τὸν Στέφανον ἄνδρες ἐυλαβεῖς καὶ ἐπόιησαντο κοπετὸν μέγαν ἐπ' ἀυτῷ.*" It was probably upon this somewhat slender foundation that the elaborate legend referred to in these lines was built by writers of the fifth century. The legend, as given in Smith's "Dict. of the Bible," vol. iii. p. 1379, was as follows:—

"The High-Priest, it is said, had intended to leave the corpse of St. Stephen to be devoured by beasts of prey. It was rescued by Gamaliel, carried off in his own chariot by night, and buried in a new tomb upon his property at Caphar Gamala = *Village of the Camel*, eight leagues from Jerusalem. The funeral lamentations lasted forty days. All the Apostles attended. Gamaliel undertook the expense, and, on his death, was interred in an adjacent cave.

"This story was probably first drawn up on the occasion of the remarkable event which occurred in A.D. 415, under the name of "the Invention and Translation of the Relics of St. Stephen." Successive visions of Gamaliel to Lucian, the parish priest of Caphar Gamala, on the 3rd and 18th of December in that year, revealed the spot where the remains of the martyr would be found.

They were identified by a tablet bearing his name *Cheliel*, and were carried in state to Jerusalem, amidst various portents, and buried in the church on Mount Zion, the scene of so many early Christian traditions."

71, 72. The legend adds, that, when they began to dig, and disturb the soil about the saint's tomb, a delightful fragrance arose therefrom, and cured seventy persons, sick of different diseases and infirmities.

Sequence XXX.

1. The rose, as though red with blood, is an emblem constantly used in Mediæval poetry for Martyrs.

4-6. Egypt, the land of darkness and tribulation to the Jews, typifies the world in bondage to Satan.

7-12. Cf. Acts vii. 56-58.

13-18. Cf. Acts vii. 59.

19-24. Cf. Acts vii. 55.

25. Grapes in the wine-press are emblems of Christ and his Martyrs in their sufferings.

Sequence XXXI.

7-9. Cf. John xiii. 23.

10, 11. Cf. John xix. 25-27.

12. Tradition represents St. John as having been throughout his whole life a pure virgin.

16-18. An allusion to the miracle by which St. John escapes martyrdom at Rome. "Jussu igitur Domitiani, Romam deducitur et deducto omnes capilli pro derisioni a capite præscinduntur, ac ante portam urbis quæ Latinam dicitur in dolium ferventis olei, igne desubter candente, mitti jubetur: nullum tamen ibidem dolorem sensit, sed penitus illæsus exivit."—*Golden Legend*, "De Johanne ante Portam Latinam."

19. This refers to the legend that, whilst in Asia, St. John drank a cup of hemlock, which was intended to cause his death, and suffered no harm from it.

25-30. Crato, a philosopher, discoursing upon the worthlessness of the things of this world, had persuaded two young men to sell all that they had, and to spend the money thus obtained in the purchase of some jewels. This being done, he induces them to break the gems in pieces, when St. John happened to pass that way, and invited the philosopher to embrace the true faith. Crato said that if St. John's Master was the true God, He could cause the broken gems to re-unite, so that the worth of them might be given to the poor. St. John then took the gems into his hands, and prayed, and they became whole once more. Upon this Crato and the two young men believed, and, selling the precious stones, gave the price of them to the poor. Two other young men, touched by this example, sold all that they possessed, employed themselves in almsgiving, and followed the Apostle. One day, seeing certain, who had been their servants once, richly clad, whilst they themselves had only an old cloak to cover them, they grew sad. Then St. John, since they were on the sea-shore, desired them to collect some bits of wood and small pebbles, and these he changed into gold and precious stones.

31-41. Our Lord with His disciples, so the legend runs, appeared to St. John, then in his ninety-ninth year, and desired him to come to Him, "For it is time," said He, "that thou shouldest sup with thy brethren at My table." On the following Lord's day accordingly, when the people were gathered in church, St. John, after exhorting them to remain steadfast in the faith, directed a tomb to be prepared for him near the altar, and descended into it. A bright light hid him from the spectators' eyes, and, when it presently cleared away, instead of finding St. John there, they found the vault full of manna, which continued to be constantly generated there ever afterwards.

SEQUENCE XXXII.

1-6. Cf. 1 John ii. 16, 17; John xii. 48.

13. Cf. Rev. i. 10.

19-48. "The poet urges that the *theology*, properly so called, belongs to St. John. The other Evangelists set forth Christ's earthly ministry of labour and toil and passion; St. John rather the relation of Him, the creative Word, to the Father,—John i. 3; Gen. i. 1,—and His return, at the end of time, *cum ultrici framea* (v. 48)—these last words containing an allusion to that sublimest of all visions, Rev. xix. 11-16." *Trench*, "Sacred Latin Poetry," pp. 73, 74.

19. Cf. Rev. xix. 12; Gen. xxxii. 20; Judges xiii. 17, 18.

36. Cf. Acts iv. 13, Vulgate: "Homines sine litteris et *idiotæ.*"

37-42. Cf. Ezek. i. 18; x. 12, as to *lumen visuale:* i. 6, 10, as to *vultus anceps:* i. 6, 9, as to *leves alæ:* i. 21, as to *rotæ stantes.*

"A difficult stanza . . . I take Adam to mean that St. John's eagle-glance, *lumen visuale*, with all else ascribed to him here, was seen in heaven, anticipated in Ezekiel's vision, before John himself, or his Lord, the charioteer, *auriga*, of that wondrous chariot, which John, with the other 'living creatures,' upbore, took form and shape on earth. But I am not satisfied with this explanation."—*Trench*, ad loc.

49, 50. Cf. Ezek. i. 19, Vulgate: "Cumque ambularent animalia, ambulabant pariter et rotæ juxta ea, et cum elevarentur animalia de terra, elevabantur simul et rotæ."

52-54. Cf. Rev. v. 8, 9.

SEQUENCE XXXIII.

This Sequence, like all those in the irregular metres common to the *Notkerian* Sequences, was probably written to be used with music previously composed.

Strophe 2. *Nuptias . . liquit.* Adam seems here to adopt the legendary notion, that the marriage at Cana in Galilee was that of St. John, and that the Apostle left the marriage-feast to follow Christ.

Strophe 5. *Virus sorrens sorbuit.* Vide note to Sequence xxxi. 19. *Vir vita refloruit et matrona.* The "Golden Legend" records that St. John raised a woman called Drusiana to life — "De S. Johanne," sec. 1.—and a young man, who had been married thirty days—sec. 4. *Ordericus Vitalis*, "Eccl. History of England and Normandy," bk. ii. cap. v., gives *Stacteus* as the name of the young man.

Aurum de frondibus, &c. Vide note to Sequence xxxi. 25-30.

Strophe 6. *Hunc vocans*, &c. Vide note to Sequence xxxi. 31-41.

SEQUENCE XXXIV.

1. "Evangelista Johannes velut aquila volat altius caliginemque terræ transcendit, et lucem veritatis firmioribus oculis intuetur."—*Augustine*, "In Evangel. Joh.," iii. 15, sec. 1. "Altissimus Evangelista Dei."—*Anselmi*, "Orat." 67.

20. *O Virgo*. Vide note on Sequence xxxi. 12.

SEQUENCE XXXV.

1. *Sion* = The Church Militant.

23, 24. A large portion of Thomas à Becket's days of exile

were, by the invitation of the King of France, spent by him in the province of Sens in France—days amongst the happiest of his life.

28. Points to the probability of the Archbishop having passed some time in the Abbey of St. Victor.

31-33. "In brevi in tantam familiaritatem a præfato rege Thomas est admissus, ut per diversas regiones se beatos reputarent qui ei ut consiliario et cancellario Domini obsecundare potuissent . . In regis palatio nullus eo potentior."—Quoted by *Gautier*, ad loc., from the legend of St. Thomas in the "Langres Breviary."

37-40. "Summo sacerdotio Thomas sublimatus
Est in virum alium subito mutatus."

Quoted by *Gautier* from the "Salisbury Breviary."

48, 49. Vide "Golden Legend," *De S. Thoma Cant.*, ss. 3-6.

53. Cf. John xv. 1, 5.

SEQUENCE XXXVI.

19. Cf. Matthew xxiii. 35: "That upon you may come all the righteous blood shed upon the earth, from the blood of righteous Abel unto the blood of Zacharias, son of Barachias, whom ye slew between *the temple and the altar.*"

24. Cf. 2 Kings ii. 23-25.

25. Cf. Matthew xxiii. 35.

29. Thomas à Becket's murder took place on December 29th, 1170—the morrow of the festival of the Holy Innocents.

52. Cf. Rev. vi. 11. *Stola* = "Gloria cœlestis." The *duplex stola* has many meanings in Christian symbolism; sometimes it means "impassibilitas et immortalitas"; sometimes *the soul and body*, which, after resurrection, are destined to a like immortality, &c.—Vide *Gautier*, ad loc.

SEQUENCE XXXVII.

1, 2. Cf. 2 Kings ii. 19-22.

3-5. Cf. 2 Kings iv. 38-41.

12. *Seir*, which is the same as Edom, is here taken to represent *Esau*.

27. *Bethel*. Gautier accepts the poet's use of "Bethel" in this passage, and has a note to explain its appropriateness; but taken in connection with the following line it would almost appear that Adam had for once made a slip from Scriptural accuracy, and confounded "Bethel" with "Bethesda."

The ancient name of Canterbury was "Durovernum Cantiorum," but "Dorobernia" or "Dorovernia" = *Dover*.

28-30. Cf. John v. 1-8.

31-35. The idea seems to be that from the number of miracles of healing of which the shrine of Becket at Canterbury became the scene, it rivalled the waters of Jordan and the pool of Siloam. Cf. 2 Kings v.; John ix. 7; Exod. xvi. 1-12.

37-40. Cf. 1 Sam. i. 24; Matth. xiv. 1-12.

51-75. I have not succeeded in tracing any of the miracles attributed to this saint, beyond the statement of them in the text. Gautier is silent as to any other authority for them.

SEQUENCE XXXVIII.

The story of St. Genevieve's life is as follows:—"About the year 430, St. Germanus of Auxerre and St. Lupus of Troyes, being on their way to England to combat the Pelagian heresy, stayed one night at Nanterre, then a village, about seven miles from Paris. The villagers assembled to see two prelates of such renown, and a little girl in the crowd attracted the notice of St. Germanus. Calling her to him, he asked the bystanders who she was, and learnt that her name was Genovefa, that she was seven years of age, and her parents' names were Severus and Gerontia. The parents were summoned at his request, and in the spirit of prophecy he bade them rejoice in the sanctity of their daughter, for that she would be the means of saving many. ·Then, addressing himself to the child, he dwelt on the high state of virginity, and engaged her to consecrate herself. The bishops then held a service in the church, and at nightfall bade Severus bring his daughter again at early dawn. Before departing St. Germanus reminded her of her promise, and giving her a brazen coin marked with the cross, bade her wear it as her only ornament, and leave gold and precious stones for the servants of the world. Henceforth miracles marked her out as the spouse of Christ; her mother was struck blind for a thoughtless blow, and only healed by the girl's supernatural gifts. Brought to the archbishop of Paris, generally supposed to have been Felix, to be formally consecrated as a virgin, he recognized her sanctity, and preferred her over the two girls who accompanied her. In the course of time her parents died, and Genovefa was taken by her godmother to live in Paris. Here she fell ill, and lay three days in a trance, in which an angel led her to see the dwellings of the just, and the rewards prepared for those who love God. . . The rumour of Attila's merciless and irresistible progress reached Paris, and the terrified citizens were for fleeing with their families and goods; but Genovefa prophesied that Paris would remain unharmed. . . Nor did the Huns reach Paris, but were diverted through the efficacy of her prayers, as after ages believed (circa 448).

"But her abstinence and self-inflicted privations are

perhaps her greatest characteristic. From her fifteenth to her fiftieth year she ate but twice a week, and then only bread of barley, or beans. Wine and strong drink were unknown to her. After her fiftieth year, by command of her bishops, she added a little fish and milk to her bread."—*Smith and Wace's* "Dict. of Christian Biography," vol. ii. pp. 632, 633.

29, 30. "To her wonder-working powers, no less than to her zeal, was due the building at Paris of what was in its beginning a humble chapel in honour of St. Denys and his companions."—*Smith and Wace's* "Dict. of Christian Biography," ii. 633.

It was during the building of this church, when the workmen employed upon it were without any means of satisfying their thirst, that the saint, taking an empty cask, prayed and made the sign of the cross over it, and the cask was immediately filled to the brim, and supplied the workmen continuously until the building was complete.

31, 32. The legend ran that a boy of four years old, who had fallen into a well, and after three hours had been taken out of it dead, was brought to St. Genevieve by his mother, and that the saint spread her cloak over the body, and by prayer restored it to life again.

37, 38. St. Genevieve, having gone one Sunday night very late to the church of St. Denys, in company with some young girls, the taper which they carried was extinguished, and her companions became alarmed at being in the dark. The saint thereupon took the taper into her hand and it was immediately re-lighted.

39, 40. This refers to a flood, caused by the river Seine overflowing its banks, which St. Genevieve was supposed to have caused to subside.

41. "In 1130, though some place it earlier, occurred the famous miracle of 'The Ardents,' commemorated Novem-

ber 26, by order of Pope Innocent II. Paris was devastated by a plague called the 'Ignis Sacer,' against which all human remedies proved futile. At last the coffin of St. Genovefa was carried in solemn procession and elevated in her church. All who pressed near it were healed, except three, who were concluded from that circumstance to be unbelievers."—*Smith and Wace's* "Dict. of Christian Biography," vol. ii., p. 634.

SEQUENCE XXXIX.

St. Agnes, a virgin either twelve or thirteen years old, was beheaded at Rome under Diocletian, after vain efforts first made to overcome her faith by vile outrage.

The legend about her relates that the prefect's son fell in love with her as she was returning from school, and, on her refusing his suit, fell ill. The father then endeavoured, first by large offers, and afterwards by threats, to force her into a union with his son, but, failing to move her, caused her to be stripped naked, and, in that condition, to be conveyed to a brothel. On her way thither our Lord caused her hair to grow to such a length as entirely to cover her nakedness, and on her arrival at the brothel she found an angel awaiting her, who first wrapped her in a robe of exceeding whiteness, and then filled the place with such dazzling light, that none dare approach her to do her harm. On coming there, the prefect's son (whom some represent as having been blinded) rushes recklessly towards the light and is suffocated by an evil spirit. At the prayer of St. Agnes he recovers, but the priests excite the heathen populace to fury at this Christian miracle, and demand her death by burning as a witch. On her being cast into a great fire the flames divide on other side, and burn the bystanders, but leave her untouched in the midst. The subprefect, one Aspasius, then orders her to be beheaded. As, seven days after her burial, her parents were watching her grave, St. Agnes appeared to them in the midst of a body of virgins, clothed in a vesture of gold, and with a lamb whiter than snow standing on her right hand. This apparition of St. Agnes was celebrated by the church on the 2nd of January.

65, 66. Constantia, a virgin, not the sister, but the daughter of Constantine, having, whilst in prayer at the tomb of St. Agnes, fallen asleep, saw in her dreams a vision of the saint, and woke up perfectly cured of a grievous leprosy with which she had been previously afflicted.

INDEX OF FIRST LINES OF THE FIRST VOLUME.

LATIN.

INDEX OF FIRST LINES OF THE FIRST VOLUME.

ENGLISH.

END OF VOL. I.

www.ingramcontent.com/pod-product-compliance
Lightning Source LLC
Chambersburg PA
CBHW031404270326
41929CB00010BA/1320
* 9 7 8 3 3 3 7 7 7 7 6 9 2 *